Sabrina Somers

A new face in the world of crochet, Sabrina discovered amigurumi back in 2014. After using a variety of different books and online videos, Sabrina taught herself how to crochet in two weeks. By the end of the same year, she was making her own patterns – and hasn't looked back! Now Sabrina is the founder of her own website, Sabrina's Crochet, and she sells her amazing amigurumi patterns here and via Etsy, Ravelry and Love Knitting. Pocket Amigurumi is her debut book.

Sabrina lives in Amsterdam, the Netherlands.

Pocket
AMIGURUMI

Acknowledgements

I would like to thank my boyfriend, Mark van Zee, for supporting and encouraging me to make my own amigurumi and to write my first book.

First published in Great Britain in 2017

Search Press Limited
Wellwood, North Farm Road,
Tunbridge Wells, Kent TN2 3DR

Text copyright © Sabrina Somers, 2017
www.sabrinasomers.com

Illustrations by Bess Harding: pages 14-24

Photographs by Paul Bricknell at Search Press Studios

Photographs and design copyright
© Search Press Ltd, 2017

ISBN: 978-1-78221-546-2

Suppliers

If you have difficulty in obtaining any of the materials and equipment mentioned in this book, then please visit the Search Press website for details of suppliers:
www.searchpress.com

Printed in China through Asia Pacific Offset

Pocket
AMIGURUMI

20 MINI MONSTERS
TO CROCHET & COLLECT

SABRINA SOMERS

SEARCH PRESS

Contents

Nymphea, page 28

Chamauda, page 44

Oscur, page 60

Gifly, page 76

Lunax, page 94

Coja, page 32

Oragai, page 36

Aquaqua, page 40

Pinsnip, page 48

Cinzouri, page 52

Kajuku, page 56

Mon-Chi, page 64

Boink, page 68

Glamastar, page 72

Felisky, page 80

Washimo, page 85

Corell, page 90

Stegoroc, page 98

Duplicorn, page 102

Longnoh, page 106

Introduction

My name is Sabrina Somers, and welcome to my first book, *Pocket Amigurumi*! This is where your journey begins, and you can start collecting your own mini monsters.

Three years ago I discovered crocheting. I saw a number of cute plushies on the internet, and decided I wanted to make them myself too. I got a crochet book and started to learn how to crochet. It caused a lot of frustration, because it wasn't as easy as it looked, but after two weeks I made my first amigurumi.

By the end of the year I had made many characters from different crochet books. I thought then it was time to design my own amigurumi.

This book contains 20 little monsters which are all quick and easy to make. If you don't know how to crochet, or just need to brush up your skills, all the crochet stitches and making-up instructions are provided at the beginning of the book. So there's no excuse not to get started on your own collection of these cute crochet monsters! Each one has its own special character, and you can try making them in different colours and mixing up their eyes, ears, wings and other features to create your own cute creatures.

Good luck, and have fun on your crochet expedition!

Before You Start Collecting

Materials

Basic Equipment

- **Scissors** to cut the yarn.
- **Felt** in different colours to make the eyes, noses and mouths. In each project I have recommended a colour to use for your monster.
- **Fabric glue** to paste the felt parts to the monsters.
- **Pins**. I recommend you pin the parts together before you sew them on.
- **Stitch markers** show where you started each rounded. For all the monsters you need to work in rounds.
- **Fine-toothed brush** – like a slicker brush – to make some parts of the monsters fluffy.
- **Jewellery wire** for shaping parts of the monsters and for providing support. I like to use wire with 1 millimetre (18 gauge) thickness, as I find it is strong yet thin enough to bend.

Hooks & needles

- For all of the monsters you will need just one hook to crochet – **size 2.5mm (UK 13/ US B-1)**.
- To sew the monsters' different parts together you will need a regular **tapestry (blunt-end) needle**.

FABRIC GLUE
Textiel lijm
Colle à textile
Textilkleber
Adhesivo textile 25 ml

2.5 mm

Yarn

- For all the monsters I use 4-ply (fine/sport weight), 100% cotton yarn; although, for some of the amigurumi creatures, 3-ply (light fingering) acrylic yarn has been used to make the tails fluffy as it is easier to brush. With several of the monsters I embroider a mouth; in these instances, I use black crochet cotton thread or black yarn.

- I have worked with a selection of crochet cotton brands: Lana Grossa Cotone (125m/137yd per 50g), Phildar Phil Coton 3 (121m/132yd per 50g), SMC Catania (125m/136yd per 50g), Katia Capri (125m/137yd per 50g) and Katia Peques (231m/253yd per 50g). For some of the mouths, I use Durable Embroidery crochet cotton 1001 (160m/175yd per 20g). All of these are available to buy online, but if you are unable to find them, any yarn of a similar weight will work just as well.

- You don't have to use the colours I specify for the monsters – to make your collection more unique, you can make the monsters in any colour you like.

- If you have started crocheting for the first time, I recommend you use lighter colours, as the stitches will be clearer to see.

Stuffing

- I use synthetic polyester toy stuffing (fiberfill), but you can use whatever type of stuffing you wish.

12

Crochet Crash Course

Even practised crocheters need to refresh their memories now and then! Here are the crochet basics you will need to create your little monsters.

Abbreviations

Both US and UK crochet abbreviations are provided. In each case the US term is given first, followed by the UK term in brackets. The abbreviations listed below are the most frequently used terms in the book.

US

sc (single crochet)
hdc (half double crochet)
dc (double crochet)
tr (treble crochet)
skip

UK

dc (double crochet)
htr (half treble crochet)
tr (treble crochet)
dtr (double treble crochet)
miss

Other terms:

ch	chain
dec	decrease
rep	repeat
sl st	slip stitch
st/sts	stitch/es
tch	turning chain

Stitches

Slip knot

Your first chain (foundation chain) starts with a slip knot – this holds your yarn securely on the hook.

1 Create a loop by making a cross on your hand.

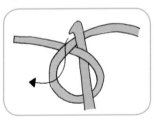

2 Go through the loop with your hook and catch the yarn.

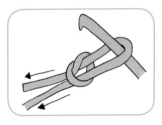

3 Pull the yarn through the loop.

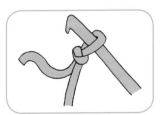

4 Pull the ends to tighten the knot.

Slip stitch

A slip stitch (sl st) is used to join different rounds, or for closing up your piece. Turn to page 23 to see this stitch being used to close up your monsters.

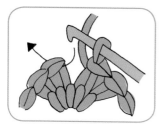

1 Insert your hook into the next whole stitch (push the hook through both the front and back loops).

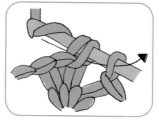

2 Wrap the yarn over the hook, and pull it through the stitch.

3 Wrap the yarn around your hook, and pull it through the loop on your hook.

Chain stitch

1 Start with a slip knot, and catch the working end of the yarn with your hook.

2 Pull the yarn through the loop on your hook. Now you've made 1 chain.

Tip
The loop on your hook doesn't count as a stitch – look for the 'V' shape after you've made your first stitch.

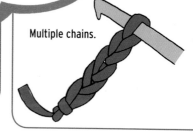

Multiple chains.

TURNING CHAIN

The turning chain is a normal chain, but includes one or two more stitches to get your yarn to the right height needed to work the first stitch of your next row/round.

After you crochet the last stitch for the final row/round, usually you turn your work around and work a chain stitch – this is your turning chain. As these monsters are mostly made with single crochet (*UK double crochet*), the turning chain is 'skipped' and not counted as a stitch. Continue with the first stitch in your next row/round.

⫸ Magic ring

All the basic spherical and tubular shapes for the monsters in this book start with a magic ring. This key stitch allows you to make 3D objects without leaving a hole in the starting round. You can then make spiral circles by working single crochet (*UK double crochet*) stitches into the ring, thus creating a spiral pattern that allows seamless joins between each round.

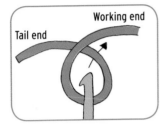

1 Create a loop by crossing the working end of the yarn (the yarn nearest the ball), then go through the loop with your hook and 'catch' the yarn.

2 Pull the yarn through the loop then catch the working end of the yarn with your hook.

3 You'll now have a loop on your hook, and the ring which you'll work into. To secure the ring, wrap the working end around your hook and pull this through the loop to make a slip stitch.

4 Start to make sc (*UK dc*) stitches into the ring. To do this, insert your hook into the ring and pull the working yarn through it; you now have 2 loops on your hook. Yarn over hook, and pull through both loops on your hook. You'll now have 1 sc (*UK dc*) worked into the ring! Most patterns in this book start with 6 sc (*UK dc*) worked into the ring.

5 Pull the tail end of the yarn to close the ring and make a small circle without a hole. You now have a magic ring.

INCREASING

Once you've made the magic ring, you'll need to make it wider with each round to make the iconic ball shape for your monsters.
In the instructions you'll see this in Round 2:

2 sc (*UK dc*) in each st to end (12 sts).

This means you increase by working 2 stitches into each stitch. You simply work another single crochet (*UK dc*) into the same stitch you've just worked into to double the number of stitches in the first round.

Single (UK Double) crochet

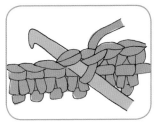

1 Insert your hook into the next stitch. Go through the front and back loops of the stitch.

2 Yarn over your hook.

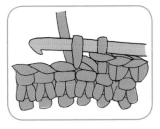

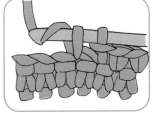

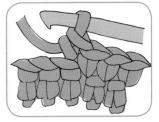

3 Pull the yarn through the stitch, so you have 2 loops on your hook.

4 Yarn over again.

5 Pull the yarn through both loops on your hook. The stitch is now complete.

Half double (UK Half treble) crochet

1 Yarn over so you have 2 loops on your hook.

2 Insert your hook into the next stitch.

3 Yarn over.

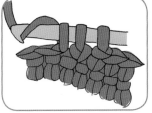

4 Pull the yarn through the stitch, so you have 3 loops on your hook.

5 Yarn over again.

6 Pull the yarn through all 3 loops on your hook.

Double (UK Treble) crochet

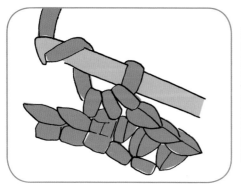

1 Yarn over so you have 2 loops on your hook.

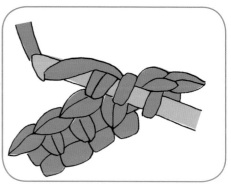

2 Insert your hook into the next stitch and yarn over again.

3 Pull yarn through the stitch, so you have 3 loops on your hook.

4 Yarn over again.

5 Pull the yarn through the first 2 loops, so you have 2 loops left on your hook.

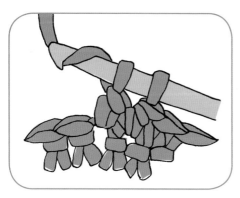

6 Yarn over once more.

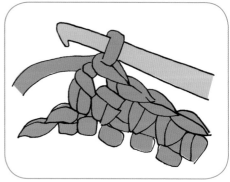

7 Pull it through the remaining loops on your hook.

Treble (UK Double treble) crochet

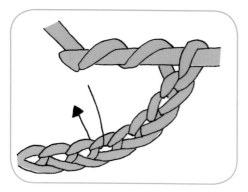

1 Here the treble (*UK double treble*) stitch is being worked into a foundation chain to make it easier to see. Yarn over twice so you have 3 loops on your hook, and insert into the fifth stitch from the hook.

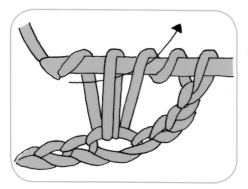

2 Yarn over and pull the loop through the stitch. You should now have 4 loops on your hook. Yarn over again, and pull this through the first 2 loops.

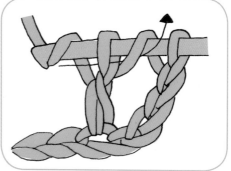

3 You will now have 3 loops left on your hook. Yarn over, and pull this through the first 2 loops.

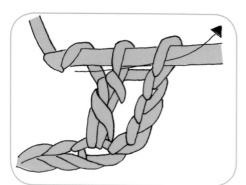

4 Now only 2 loops remain! Yarn over again, and pull this through the last 2 loops.

5 You have now made 1 treble (*UK double treble*) crochet.

Techniques

Tip

In crochet you have 'right' and 'wrong' sides – the 'right' side in amigurumi is the exterior, and the 'wrong' side is the interior.

Front & back loops

Front loop

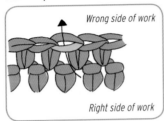

Wrong side of work

Right side of work

Back loop

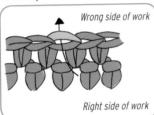

Wrong side of work

Right side of work

Normally in crochet you go through the 'whole stitch', which means you go through both loops of the chain. But in some patterns, like amigurumi, you need to go only in the front loop or back loop.

Front and back loops play an important part in making your amigurumi monsters: crocheting into either the front or back loops on the body leaves open 'rings' to attach arms and legs, making it much easier to sew on arms, legs, wings and other appendages later.

Front loops are also important for making invisible decreases in your amigurumi. The usual way to decrease is sc2tog/single crochet 2 together (*UK dc2tog/double crochet 2 together*), but in rounds this method can lead to gaps and bumps. With an invisible decrease (see opposite) any bulges in your work stay inside, leaving the outside smoother and neater.

Switching colours

1 Insert hook into the next stitch and yarn over.

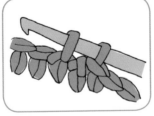

2 Pull the yarn through the stitch, so you have 2 loops on your hook.

3 Loop the new colour over your hook.

4 Pull it through the 2 loops on your hook. You have now made your first sc (*UK dc*) in the new colour.

5 Continue with your pattern in the new colour.

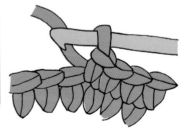

>>> Invisible decrease OR decreasing when working in rounds

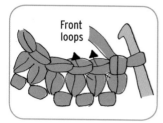

Front loops

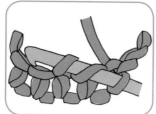

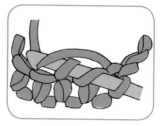

1 You will be working into the front loops only of the next 2 stitches nearest your hook.

2 Slip your hook through these 2 stitches so you have 3 loops on your hook.

3 Yarn over hook, and pull it through the first 2 stitches on your hook.

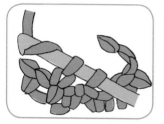

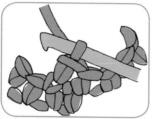

4 Yarn over hook once more, and pull this through the 2 remaining loops on your hook.

5 You should now have 1 loop on your hook, and your first invisible decrease.

>>> Decreasing when working in rows

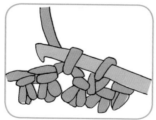

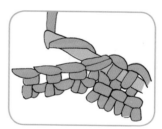

1 Go through the stitch nearest your hook and yarn over.

2 Pull the yarn through the stitch, so you have 2 loops on your hook.

3 Go through the next stitch and yarn over again.

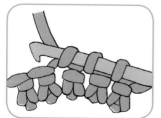

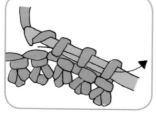

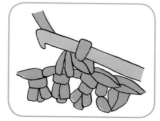

4 Pull the yarn through the stitch, so you have 3 loops on your hook.

5 Yarn over once more, and pull the yarn through all 3 loops on your hook.

6 You should now have 1 loop on your hook and your first decrease.

Making Up & Stuffing

Once you've made all the different body parts of your monster, you can start putting them all together to create your final little creature.

Stuffing

The pattern will tell you when you need to fill a body part. Put enough filling material into the part to make it smooth (**1**). Make sure that you don't fill it too much, because the stuffing will show through the stitches.

Sometimes you need to fill a part which is too small to fill by hand. You can use a pencil, crochet hook or another small object to push the stuffing into the body part (**2**).

Washimo, page 85

Closing up your work

Once you have finished working on a particular body part of your monster and stuffed it with filling material, you will need to neatly close up the hole. If you are sewing a mouth onto the head of your amigurumi, make sure you do this before closing up!

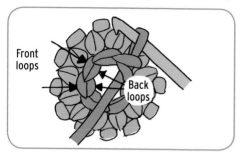

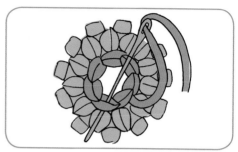

1 Before you can close your work you need to tie off. You do this by working a slip stitch. Cut the yarn, leaving a long tail end. Remember the front and back loops? To close up your work, you need to work through the front loops only.

2 Thread the tail of the yarn onto a tapestry (blunt-end) needle. Insert the needle under the front loop of the next stitch – you are working from the centre outwards. Pull the yarn taut.

3 Repeat this process all the way around, until you've worked through all the stitches at the top. For amigurumi, there are usually 6 remaining stitches.

4 Pull the yarn and, like the magic ring, this will make the hole in the middle close up. You'll notice there will be a small bump, but we'll get rid of this in a moment.

5 Push the needle, with the yarn still threaded, through the middle of the piece. Push it all the way to the other side, and bring out a little way from your piece.

6 Pull the yarn taut – the bump should now disappear. Snip close to the edge and the yarn will disappear inside your work.

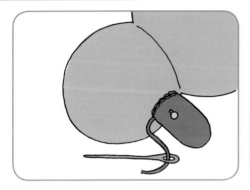

1 Pin the arm to the body and thread the tail end of the yarn through a tapestry (blunt-end) needle.

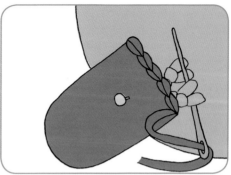

2 Insert the needle into the stitch on the body, nearest to where the tail end of the yarn is attached, and pull through.

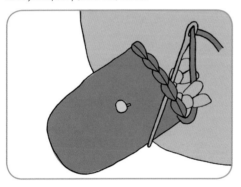

3 Insert the needle into the next stitch on the arm and pull through.

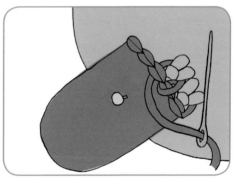

4 Now go through the second stitch again (where the yarn came out of the body) and bring the needle out of the third stitch, all the way round.

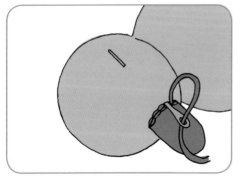

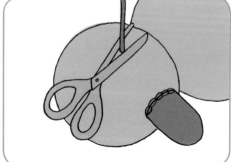

5 When you go through the last stitch, bring the needle out a fair distance away from your last stitch. Pull tight and snip the yarn close to the surface; the cut end will retract back inside the body.

Making the eyes

All of the eyes in this book are made using felt. Using the photo of your chosen monster as a guide, or by placing the photocopied or scanned printed templates provided in the book, cut out the shapes in felt. Simply paste them onto one another, and then onto your monster's head.

Making the mouth

Several of the monsters have felt mouths. Following a similar process as above – using the photo as a guide, or a photocopied or printed out scan of the template provided – cut out the mouth in felt. These are then pasted onto one another, then onto your monster's head.

> ### Tip
> If you are sewing on the mouth, make sure to do this *before* closing up the head and sewing it onto the body!

Other monsters have sewn-on mouths, and these are made with the black crochet cotton thread or 4-ply black yarn.

1 First decide where you want to put the mouth – especially with the lighter colours it is important that you put the mouth in the right place and don't move it, as the black thread can stain the yarn beneath.

2 Thread your needle. Because of the possible staining, I recommend pushing the needle through an area where you don't see the thread end, such as the place where you paste the eye. Enter the head here, and let the yarn come out of the stitch where the mouth should begin.

3 Push the needle and thread into the stitch where the mouth will end. Pull the thread out through the stitch where you first started; tie a knot, and push the knot and remaining thread into the head. Pull the mouth down in the middle for a smile.

If you like, you can put a little fabric glue under the embroidered mouth to hold it in place. To make sure you don't use too much glue, I recommend putting a little bit on an old needle, and using this to apply it to your work.

The Monsters

Nymphea

Materials:

4-ply (fine/sport weight) cotton yarn
  deep pink, 1 x 50g (1³/₄oz) ball
  light pink, 1 x 50g (1³/₄oz) ball
  yellow, small amount
  black, small amount
Stuffing (fiberfill)
Black, white and pink felt

Tools:

2.5mm (UK 13/US B-1) crochet hook
Tapestry (blunt-end) needle

Templates:

Eyes

Black

White

Cheeks

Pink

Difficulty

No difficult stitches. Only need sc (*UK dc*), sl st and ch.

Instructions:

Unless stated otherwise, all sections/body parts begin with a magic ring (see page 16 for instructions); the first round should be worked into the ring.

Head/body

Use deep pink yarn.

Round 1: 6 sc (*UK dc*) in magic ring (6 sts).

Round 2: 2 sc (*UK dc*) in each st to end (12 sts).

Round 3: *1 sc (*UK dc*) in next st, 2 sc (*UK dc*) in next st; rep from * to end (18 sts).

Round 4: *1 sc (*UK dc*) in next 2 sts, 2 sc (*UK dc*) in next st; rep from * to end (24 sts).

Round 5: *1 sc (*UK dc*) in next 3 sts, 2 sc (*UK dc*) in next st; rep from * to end (30 sts).

Round 6: *1 sc (*UK dc*) in next 4 sts, 2 sc (*UK dc*) in next st; rep from * to end (36 sts).

Round 7: *1 sc (*UK dc*) in next 5 sts, 2 sc (*UK dc*) in next st; rep from * to end (42 sts).

Round 8: *1 sc (*UK dc*) in next 6 sts, 2 sc (*UK dc*) in next st; rep from * to end (48 sts).

Round 9: *1 sc (*UK dc*) in next 7 sts, 2 sc (*UK dc*) in next st; rep from * to end (54 sts).

Rounds 10–18: 1 sc (*UK dc*) in each st to end.

Round 19: *1 sc (*UK dc*) in next 7 sts, dec over next 2 sts; rep from * to end (48 sts).

Round 20: *1 sc (*UK dc*) in next 6 sts, dec over next 2 sts; rep from * to end (42 sts).

Round 21: *1 sc (*UK dc*) in next 5 sts, dec over next 2 sts; rep from * to end (36 sts).

Round 22: *1 sc (*UK dc*) in next 4 sts, dec over next 2 sts; rep from * to end (30 sts).

Round 23: *1 sc (*UK dc*) in next 3 sts, dec over next 2 sts; rep from * to end (24 sts).

Round 24: *1 sc (*UK dc*) in next 2 sts, dec over next 2 sts; rep from * to end (18 sts).

Round 25: As Round 4 (24 sts).

Rounds 26–30: 1 sc (*UK dc*) in each st to end.

Embroider the mouth (see opposite) and fill the head/body. Tie off with a sl st, and leave enough yarn to sew the body to the leaves.

Leaves (x8)

Use light pink yarn.

Round 1: 6 sc (*UK dc*) in magic ring (6 sts).

Round 2: 1 sc (*UK dc*) in each st to end.

Round 3: *1 sc (*UK dc*) in next st, 2 sc (*UK dc*) in next st; rep from * to end (9 sts).

Round 4: As Round 2.

Round 5: *1 sc (*UK dc*) in next 2 sts, 2 sc (*UK dc*) in next st; rep from * to end (12 sts).

Round 6: As Round 2.

Round 7: *1 sc (*UK dc*) in next 3 sts, 2 sc (*UK dc*) in next st; rep from * to end (15 sts).

Round 8: As Round 2.

Round 9: *1 sc (*UK dc*) in next 4 sts, 2 sc (*UK dc*) in next st; rep from * to end (18 sts).

Rounds 10–13: As Round 2.

Round 14: *1 sc (*UK dc*) in next st, dec over next 2 sts; rep from * to end (12 sts).

Round 15: As Round 2.

Round 16: *Dec over next 2 sts; rep from * to end (6 sts).

Tie off with a sl st, and leave enough yarn to sew the leaves together.

Arms (x2)

Use deep pink yarn.

Round 1: 6 sc (*UK dc*) in magic ring
(6 sts).

Rounds 2–5: 1 sc (*UK dc*) in each st
to end.

Fill the arms. Tie off with a sl st, and
leave enough yarn to sew the arms
to the body.

Stamen (x3)

Use yellow yarn.

Row 1: 10 ch + 1 tch.

Row 2: Skip tch, 1 sl st in each ch to
end (10 sts).

Tie off, and leave enough yarn to sew
the stamen to the head.

Putting all the parts together

Sew the tops of 4 leaves together. Repeat with the
remaining leaves, and then sew them on top of the
other 4 leaves.

Sew leaves to the bottom of the body.

Sew the arms to the body, about 3 rounds below
the neck.

Sew the stamen to the top of the head.

Face

Cut 2 eyes out of black and white felt and paste these
onto the head, at approximately Round 11, with 5
stitches between the eyes.

Embroider a mouth on the head with black yarn, at
approximately Round 18. Make sure you do this before
you close up the body.

Cut 2 cheeks out of pink felt and paste these onto the
head, at approximately Round 18.

Coja

Materials:

4-ply (fine/sport weight) cotton yarn
   beige, 1 x 50g (1^3/$_4$oz) ball
   dark green, 1 x 50g (1^3/$_4$oz) ball
Crochet cotton thread, black
Stuffing (fiberfill)
Jewellery wire, 1mm (18 gauge) thick
Black and white felt

Tools:

2.5mm (UK 13/US B-1) crochet hook
Tapestry (blunt-end) needle

Templates:

Eyes

Black

White

Nose

Black

Difficulty

No difficult stitches. To get the shape of the legs, it is important to follow the instructions for increase and decrease in specific stitches.

Instructions:

Unless stated otherwise, all sections/body parts begin with a magic ring (see page 16 for instructions); the first round should be worked into the ring.

Head

Use beige yarn.

Round 1: 6 sc (*UK dc*) in magic ring (6 sts).

Round 2: 2 sc (*UK dc*) in each st to end (12 sts).

Round 3: *1 sc (*UK dc*) in next st, 2 sc (*UK dc*) in next st; rep from * to end (18 sts).

Round 4: *1 sc (*UK dc*) in next 2 sts, 2 sc (*UK dc*) in next st; rep from * to end (24 sts).

Round 5: *1 sc (*UK dc*) in next 3 sts, 2 sc (*UK dc*) in next st; rep from * to end (30 sts).

Round 6: *1 sc (*UK dc*) in next 4 sts, 2 sc (*UK dc*) in next st; rep from * to end (36 sts).

Round 7: 1 sc (*UK dc*) in each st to end.

Round 8: *1 sc (*UK dc*) in next 5 sts, 2 sc (*UK dc*) in next st; rep from * to end (42 sts).

Rounds 9–10: As Round 7.

Round 11: *1 sc (*UK dc*) in next 6 sts, 2 sc (*UK dc*) in next st; rep from * to end (48 sts).

Rounds 12–16: As Round 7.

Round 17: *1 sc (*UK dc*) in next 6 sts, dec over next 2 sts; rep from * to end (42 sts).

Round 18: *1 sc (*UK dc*) in next 5 sts, dec over next 2 sts; rep from * to end (36 sts).

Round 19: *1 sc (*UK dc*) in next 4 sts, dec over next 2 sts; rep from * to end (30 sts).

Round 20: *1 sc (*UK dc*) in next 3 sts, dec over next 2 sts; rep from * to end (24 sts).

Round 21: *1 sc (*UK dc*) in next 2 sts, dec over next 2 sts; rep from * to end (18 sts).

Fill the head and embroider the mouth (see page 35). Tie off with a sl st, and leave enough yarn to sew the head to the body.

Body

Use beige yarn.

Work Rounds 1–4 as for head.

Rounds 5–17: 1 sc (*UK dc*) in each st to end.

Round 18: *1 sc (*UK dc*) in next 2 sts, dec over next 2 sts; rep from * to end (18 sts).

Fill the body and keep filling until the last round.

Round 19: *1 sc (*UK dc*) in next st, dec over next 2 sts; rep from * to end (12 sts).

Round 20: *Dec over next 2 sts; rep from * to end (6 sts).

Tie off with a sl st and close the body.

Ears (x2)

Use dark green yarn.

Round 1: 6 sc (*UK dc*) in magic ring (6 sts).

Round 2: 1 sc (*UK dc*) in each st to end.

Round 3: *1 sc (*UK dc*) in next st, 2 sc (*UK dc*) in next st; rep from * to end (9 sts).

Round 4: As Round 2.

Round 5: *1 sc (*UK dc*) in next 2 sts, 2 sc (*UK dc*) in next st; rep from * to end (12 sts).

Round 6: As Round 2.

Round 7: As Round 3 (18 sts).

Rounds 8–13: As Round 2.

Round 14: *1 sc (*UK dc*) in next st, dec over next 2 sts; rep from * to end (12 sts).

Round 15: As Round 2.

Tie off with a sl st, and leave enough yarn to sew the ears to the head.

Forelegs (x2)

Use beige yarn.

Round 1: 6 sc (*UK dc*) in magic ring (6 sts).

Round 2: *2 sc (*UK dc*) in each of next 2 sts, 1 sc (*UK dc*) in next st; rep from * to end (10 sts).

Round 3: 1 sc (*UK dc*) in each st to end.

Round 4: [Dec over next 2 sts] twice, 1 sc (*UK dc*) in each st to end (8 sts).

Round 5: As Round 3.

Round 6: *1 sc (*UK dc*) in next 3 sts, 2 sc (*UK dc*) in next st; rep from * to end (10 sts).

Round 7: As Round 3.

Fill the legs. Tie off with a sl st, and leave enough yarn to sew the legs to the body.

Hind legs (x2)

Use beige yarn.

Work Rounds 1–5 as for forelegs.

Round 6: *1 sc (*UK dc*) in next st, 2sc (*UK dc*) in next st; rep from * to end (12 sts).

Rounds 7 and 8: As Round 3.

Fill the legs. Tie off with a sl st, and leave enough yarn to sew the legs to the body.

Tail

Use dark green yarn.

Work Rounds 1–6 as for ears.

Round 7: *1 sc (UK dc) in next 3 sts, 2 sc (UK dc) in next st; rep from * to end (15 sts).

Round 8: As Round 2.

Round 9: *1 sc (UK dc) in next 4 sts, 2 sc (UK dc) in next st; rep from * to end (18 sts).

Round 10: As Round 2.

Round 11: *1 sc (UK dc) in next 5 sts, 2 sc (UK dc) in next st; rep from * to end (21 sts).

Round 12: As Round 2.

Round 13: *1 sc (UK dc) in next 6 sts, 2 sc (UK dc) in next st; rep from * to end (24 sts).

Round 14: As Round 2.

Round 15: *1 sc (UK dc) in next 7 sts, 2 sc (UK dc) in next st; rep from * to end (27 sts).

Round 16: As Round 2.

Round 17: *1 sc (UK dc) in next 8 sts, 2 sc (UK dc) in next st; rep from * to end (30 sts).

Rounds 18–20: As Round 2.

Round 21: *1 sc (UK dc) in next 3 sts, dec over next 2 sts; rep from * to end (24 sts).

Round 22: As Round 2.

Round 23: *1 sc (UK dc) in next 2 sts, dec over next 2 sts; rep from * to end (18 sts).

Round 24: *1 sc (UK dc) in next st, dec over next 2 sts; rep from * to end (12 sts).

Round 25: *Dec over next 2 sts; rep from * to end (6 sts).

Rounds 26–30: As Round 2.

Insert some jewellery wire into the tail, and bend it into your chosen shape.

Tie off with a sl st, and leave enough yarn to sew the tail to the body.

Collar

Use dark green yarn.

Row 1: 24 ch + 1 tch.

Row 2: Skip tch, *1 sl st in next ch, work 3 ch + 1 tch, skip tch, 1 sl st in next ch of 3-ch, 1 sc (UK dc) in next 2 ch of 3-ch , skip next ch of original chain, 1 sl st in next ch; rep from * seven more times, until you have 8 rounded points on a strip and all ch have been worked.

Tie off, and leave enough yarn to sew the ends together

Putting all the parts together

Sew the head to the body, at approximately Round 5.

Sew the ears to the head, at approximately Round 6.

Sew the legs to the body, the forelegs at approximately Round 5 and the hind legs at Round 13.

Place the collar around the neck, press it to your monster and sew the ends together.

Sew the tail to the back of the body.

Face

Cut 2 eyes out of black and white felt and paste these onto the head, at approximately Round 9, with 5 stitches between the eyes.

Cut a nose out of black felt and paste it onto the head, at approximately Round 14.

Embroider a mouth on the head with black crochet cotton thread, at approximately Round 16. Make sure you do this before you close up the head.

Oragai

What you need:

Materials:

4-ply (fine/sport weight) cotton yarn
  light yellow, 1 x 50g ($1^3/_4$oz) ball
  yellow, 1 x 50g ($1^3/_4$oz) ball
  brown, small amount
Stuffing (fiberfill)
Black, white and red felt

Tools:

2.5mm (UK 13/US B-1) crochet hook
Tapestry (blunt-end) needle

Templates:

Eyes

Black

White

Mouth

Black

Red

Difficulty

To get the shape of the feet, it is important to follow the instructions for increase and decrease in specific stitches. For the ears it is also important to follow the rows carefully.

Instructions:

Unless stated otherwise, all sections/body parts begin with a magic ring (see page 16 for instructions); the first round should be worked into the ring.

Head/body

Use light yellow yarn.

Round 1: 6 sc (*UK dc*) in magic ring (6 sts).

Round 2: 2 sc (*UK dc*) in each st to end (12 sts).

Round 3: *1 sc (*UK dc*) in next st, 2 sc (*UK dc*) in next st; rep from * to end (18 sts).

Round 4: *1 sc (*UK dc*) in next 2 sts, 2 sc (*UK dc*) in next st; rep from * to end (24 sts).

Round 5: *1 sc (*UK dc*) in next 3 sts, 2 sc (*UK dc*) in next st; rep from * to end (30 sts).

Round 6: *1 sc (*UK dc*) in next 4 sts, 2 sc (*UK dc*) in next st; rep from * to end (36 sts).

Round 7: *1 sc (*UK dc*) in next 5 sts, 2 sc (*UK dc*) in next st; rep from * to end (42 sts).

Round 8: *1 sc (*UK dc*) in next 6 sts, 2 sc (*UK dc*) in next st; rep from * to end (48 sts).

Round 9: *1 sc (*UK dc*) in next 7 sts, 2 sc (*UK dc*) in next st; rep from * to end (54 sts).

Rounds 10–18: 1 sc (*UK dc*) in each st to end.

Round 19: *1 sc (*UK dc*) in next 7 sts, dec over next 2 sts; rep from * to end (48 sts).

Round 20: *1 sc (*UK dc*) in next 6 sts, dec over next 2 sts; rep from * to end (42 sts).

Round 21: *1 sc (*UK dc*) in next 5 sts, dec over next 2 sts; rep from * to end (36 sts).

Round 22: *1 sc (*UK dc*) in next 4 sts, dec over next 2 sts; rep from * to end (30 sts).

Round 23: *1 sc (*UK dc*) in next 3 sts, dec over next 2 sts; rep from * to end (24 sts).

Round 24: *1 sc (*UK dc*) in next 2 sts, dec over next 2 sts; rep from * to end (18 sts).

Fill the head/body, and keep filling until the last round.

Rounds 25 and 26: As Rounds 4 and 5 (30 sts).

Rounds 27 and 28: As Round 18.

Switch to yellow yarn.

Rounds 29–31: As Round 18.

Rounds 32 and 33: As Rounds 23 and 24 (18 sts).

Round 34: *1 sc (*UK dc*) in next st, dec over next 2 sts; rep from * to end (12 sts).

Round 35: *Dec over next 2 sts; rep from * to end (6 sts).

Tie off with a sl st and close the head/body.

Arms (x2)

Use yellow yarn.

Round 1: 6 sc (*UK dc*) in magic ring (6 sts).

Round 2: *1 sc (*UK dc*) in next st, 2 sc (*UK dc*) in next st; rep from * to end (9 sts).

Round 3: 1 sc (*UK dc*) in each st to end.

Switch to light yellow yarn.

Rounds 4–6: As Round 3.

Fill the arms. Tie off with a sl st, and leave enough yarn to sew the arms to the body.

Feet (x2)

Use brown yarn.

Round 1: 6 sc (*UK dc*) in magic ring (6 sts).

Round 2: *2 sc (*UK dc*) in each of next 2 sts, 1 sc (*UK dc*) in next st; rep from * to end (10 sts).

Switch to yellow yarn.

Round 3: *1 sc (*UK dc*) in next st, 2 sc (*UK dc*) in each of next 2 sts, 1 sc (*UK dc*) in next 2 sts; rep from * to end (14 sts).

Round 4: 1 sc (*UK dc*) in each st to end.

Round 5: 1 sc (*UK dc*) in next st, [dec over next 2 sts] twice, 1 sc (*UK dc*) in each st to end (12 sts).

Round 6: *1 sc (*UK dc*) in next 2 sts, dec over next 2 sts; rep from * to end (9 sts).

Fill the feet. Tie off with a sl st, and leave enough yarn to sew the feet to the body.

Tail

Use yellow yarn.

Work Rounds 1 and 2 as for head/body.

Round 3: *1 sc (*UK dc*) in next 3 sts, 2 sc (*UK dc*) in next st; rep from * to end (15 sts).

Rounds 4 and 5: 1 sc (*UK dc*) in each st to end.

Round 6: *1 sc (*UK dc*) in next st, dec over next 2 sts; rep from * to end (10 sts).

Fill the tail. Tie off with a sl st, and leave enough yarn to sew the tail to the body.

Ears (x4)

Use yellow yarn. Turn work at the end of each row.

Row 1: 8 ch + 1 tch.

Row 2: Skip tch, 1 sc (*UK dc*) in each ch to end (8 sts).

Row 3: 1 tch, 1 sc (*UK dc*) in next 6 sts, dec over last 2 sts (7 sts).

Row 4: 1 tch, dec over next 2 sts, 1 sc (*UK dc*) in each st to end (6 sts).

Row 5: 1 tch, 1 sc (*UK dc*) in next 3 sts, turn (leaving remaining sts unworked) (3 sts).

Row 6: 1 tch, 1 sc (*UK dc*) in next 3 sts, 3 ch + 1 tch.

Row 7: Skip tch, 1 sc (*UK dc*) in next 3 ch, 1 sc (*UK dc*) in next 3 sts (6 sts).

Row 8: 1 tch, 1 sc (*UK dc*) in each st to end.

Row 9: As Row 5 (3 sts).

Row 10: As Row 4 (2 sts).

Row 11: As Row 8.

Hold 2 ear pieces together and work a row of sc (*UK dc*) around entire edge to join. Repeat for other ear. Leave enough yarn to sew the ears to the head.

Putting all the parts together

Sew the feet to the body, approximately 6 rounds below the neck.

Sew the arms to the body, approximately 2 rounds below the neck.

Sew the tail to the body, approximately 5 rounds below the neck.

Sew the ears to the head, at approximately Round 6.

Face

Cut 2 eyes out of black and white felt and paste these onto the head, at approximately Round 12, with 6 stitches between the eyes.

Cut a mouth out of black and red felt and paste it onto the head, at approximately Round 17.

Aquaqua

Materials:

4-ply (fine/sport weight) cotton yarn
   blue, 1 x 50g (1³/₄oz) ball
   medium grey, 1 x 50g (1³/₄oz) ball
   light blue, small amount
Stuffing (fiberfill)
Black and white felt
Jewellery wire, 1mm (18 gauge) thick

Tools:

2.5mm (UK 13/US B-1) crochet hook
Tapestry (blunt-end) needle

Templates:

Eyes

Black   White   White

Difficulty

🦆 🦆 🦆 🦆 🦆

The beak and swim ring
are a little bit more
difficult because they
require dc (*UK tr*).

Instructions:

Unless stated otherwise, all sections/body parts begin
with a magic ring (see page 16 for instructions); the first
round should be worked into the ring.

Head/body

Use blue yarn.

Round 1: 6 sc (*UK dc*) in magic ring (6 sts).

Round 2: 2 sc (*UK dc*) in each st to end (12 sts).

Round 3: *1 sc (*UK dc*) in next st, 2 sc (*UK dc*) in next st;
rep from * to end (18 sts).

Round 4: *1 sc (*UK dc*) in next 2 sts, 2 sc (*UK dc*) in next
st; rep from * to end (24 sts).

Round 5: *1 sc (*UK dc*) in next 3 sts, 2 sc (*UK dc*) in next
st; rep from * to end (30 sts).

Round 6: *1 sc (*UK dc*) in next 4 sts, 2 sc (*UK dc*) in next
st; rep from * to end (36 sts).

Round 7: *1 sc (*UK dc*) in next 5 sts, 2 sc (*UK dc*) in next
st; rep from * to end (42 sts).

Round 8: *1 sc (*UK dc*) in next 6 sts, 2 sc (*UK dc*) in next
st; rep from * to end (48 sts).

Rounds 9–16: 1 sc (*UK dc*) in each st to end.

Round 17: *1 sc (*UK dc*) in next 6 sts, dec over next 2
sts; rep from * to end (42 sts).

Round 18: *1 sc (*UK dc*) in next 5 sts, dec over next 2
sts; rep from * to end (36 sts).

Round 19: *1 sc (*UK dc*) in next 4 sts, dec over next 2
sts; rep from * to end (30 sts).

Round 20: *1 sc (*UK dc*) in next 3 sts, dec over next 2
sts; rep from * to end (24 sts).

Round 21: *1 sc (*UK dc*) in next 2 sts, dec over next 2
sts; rep from * to end (18 sts).

Fill the head/body and keep filling until the last round.

Round 22: As Round 4 (24 sts).

Round 23: As Round 16.

Round 24: As Round 5 (30 sts).

Round 25: As Round 16.

Round 26: As Round 6 (36 sts).

Rounds 27–31: As Round 16.

Round 32–34: As Rounds 19–21 (18 sts).

Round 35: *1 sc (*UK dc*) in next st, dec over next 2 sts; rep from * to end (12 sts).

Round 36: *Dec over next 2 sts; rep from * to end (6 sts).

Tie off with a sl st and close the head/body.

Arms (x2)

Use blue yarn.

Round 1: 6 sc (*UK dc*) in magic ring (6 sts).

Round 2: *1 sc (*UK dc*) in next st, 2 sc (*UK dc*) in next st; rep from * to end (9 sts).

Switch to light blue yarn.

Round 3: 1 sc (*UK dc*) in each st to end.

Round 4: *1 sc (*UK dc*) in next 2 sts, 2 sc (*UK dc*) in next st; rep from * to end (12 sts).

Return to blue yarn.

Rounds 5–7: As Round 3.

Fill the arms. Tie off with a sl st, and leave enough yarn to sew the arms to the body.

Feet (x2)

Use medium grey yarn.

Work Rounds 1 and 2 as for head/body.

Rounds 3–7: 1 sc (*UK dc*) in each st to end.

Round 8: *Dec over next 2 sts; rep from * to end (6 sts).

Tie off with a sl st and close the feet. Leave enough yarn to sew the feet to the body.

Swim ring

Use light blue yarn.

Row 1: 45 ch + 1 tch.

Row 2: Turn work, skip tch, *1 sl st in next ch, 1 dc (*UK tr*) in next 3 ch, 1 sl st in next ch; rep from * eight more times, until you have 9 rounded points on a strip and all ch have been worked.

Tie off, and leave enough yarn to sew the swim ring to the body.

Beak

Use medium grey yarn.

Work Rounds 1–4 as for head/body.

Rounds 5–11: 1 sc (*UK dc*) in each st to end.

Round 12: Working in the front loops only, 1 sc (*UK dc*) in next st, 1 hdc (*UK htr*) in next 2 sts, 1 dc (*UK tr*) in next 2 sts, 1 hdc (*UK htr*) in next 2 sts, 1 sc (*UK dc*) in next st. Leave remaining sts unworked.

Tie off with a sl st, and leave enough yarn to sew the beak to the head.

Tail

Use medium grey yarn.

Work Rounds 1–4 as for head/body.

Rounds 5–7: 1 sc (*UK dc*) in each st to end.

Switch to blue yarn.

Rounds 8–9: As Round 7.

Return to medium grey yarn.

Rounds 10–13: As Round 7.

Round 14: *1 sc (*UK dc*) in next 6 sts, dec over next 2 sts; rep from * to end (21 sts).

Rounds 15 and 16: As Round 7.

Round 17: *1 sc (*UK dc*) in next 5 sts, dec over next 2 sts; rep from * to end (18 sts).

Rounds 18 and 19: As Round 7.

Round 20: *1 sc (*UK dc*) in next 4 sts, dec over next 2 sts; rep from * to end (15 sts).

Rounds 21 and 22: As Round 7.

Round 23: *1 sc (*UK dc*) in next 3 sts, dec over next 2 sts; rep from * to end (12 sts).

Round 24: As Round 7.

Insert some jewellery wire into the tail and bend it into your chosen shape.

Tie off with a sl st, and leave enough yarn to sew the tail to the body.

Putting all the parts together

Sew the arms to the body, approximately 2 rounds below the neck.

Sew the feet to the bottom of the body.

Place the swim ring around the body, and sew it approximately 7 rounds below the neck.

Sew the beak to the head, at approximately Round 14.

Sew the tail to the body, approximately 12 rounds below the neck.

Face

Cut 2 eyes out of black and white felt and paste these onto the head, at approximately Round 10, with 8 stitches between the eyes.

Chamauda

What you need:

Materials:

4-ply (fine/sport weight) cotton yarn
dark gold, 1 x 50g (1³/₄oz) ball
light yellow, 1 x 50g (1³/₄oz) ball
3-ply (light fingering) acrylic yarn
yellow, 1 x 50g (1³/₄oz) ball
red, 1 x 50g (1³/₄oz) ball
Stuffing (fiberfill)
Black, white and brown felt

Tools:

2.5mm (UK 13/US B-1) crochet hook
Tapestry (blunt-end) needle
Fine-toothed brush, like a slicker brush

Templates:

Eyes

White   Black   White

Nose

          Brown

Difficulty

For the whiskers you
need to know dc (*UK tr*).
To get the shape of the
belly, it is important to
follow the instructions for
increase and decrease in
specific stitches.

Instructions:

Unless stated otherwise, all sections/body parts begin
with a magic ring (see page 16 for instructions); the first
round should be worked into the ring.

Head/body

Use dark gold yarn.

Round 1: 6 sc (*UK dc*) in magic ring (6 sts).

Round 2: 2 sc (*UK dc*) in each st to end (12 sts).

Round 3: *1 sc (*UK dc*) in next st, 2 sc (*UK dc*) in next st;
rep from * to end (18 sts).

Round 4: *1 sc (*UK dc*) in next 2 sts, 2 sc (*UK dc*) in next
st; rep from * to end (24 sts).

Round 5: *1 sc (*UK dc*) in next 3 sts, 2 sc (*UK dc*) in next
st; rep from * to end (30 sts).

Round 6: *1 sc (*UK dc*) in next 4 sts, 2 sc (*UK dc*) in next
st; rep from * to end (36 sts).

Round 7: *1 sc (*UK dc*) in next 5 sts, 2 sc (*UK dc*) in next
st; rep from * to end (42 sts).

Round 8: *1 sc (*UK dc*) in next 6 sts, 2 sc (*UK dc*) in next
st; rep from * to end (48 sts).

Rounds 9–16: 1 sc (*UK dc*) in each st to end.

Round 17: *1 sc (*UK dc*) in next 6 sts, dec over next 2
sts; rep from * to end (42 sts).

Round 18: *1 sc (*UK dc*) in next 5 sts, dec over next 2
sts; rep from * to end (36 sts).

Round 19: *1 sc (*UK dc*) in next 4 sts, dec over next 2
sts; rep from * to end (30 sts).

Round 20: *1 sc (*UK dc*) in next 3 sts, dec over next 2
sts; rep from * to end (24 sts).

Round 21: *1 sc (*UK dc*) in next 2 sts, dec over next 2
sts; rep from * to end (18 sts).

Fill the head/body and keep filling until the last round.

Round 22: As Round 4 (24 sts).

Round 23: As Round 16.

Round 24: As Round 5 (30 sts).

Rounds 25–31: As Round 16.

Rounds 32 and 33: As Rounds 20 and 21 (18 sts).

Round 34: *1 sc (*UK dc*) in next st, dec over next 2 sts; rep from * to end (12 sts).

Round 35: *Dec over next 2 sts; rep from * to end (6 sts).

Tie off with a sl st and close the head/body.

Belly

Use light yellow yarn.

Work Rounds 1 and 2 as for head/body.

Round 3: *2 sc (*UK dc*) in each of next 3 sts, 1 sc (*UK dc*) in next 3 sts; rep from * to end (18 sts).

Tie off with a sl st, and leave enough yarn to sew the belly to the body.

Arms (x2)

Use dark gold yarn.

Round 1: 6 sc (*UK dc*) in magic ring (6 sts).

Round 2: *1 sc (*UK dc*) in next st, 2 sc (*UK dc*) in next st; rep from * to end (9 sts).

Rounds 3–6: 1 sc (*UK dc*) in each st to end.

Fill the arms. Tie off with a sl st, and leave enough yarn to sew the arms to the body.

Legs (x2)

Use dark gold yarn.

Work Rounds 1 and 2 as for head/body.

Round 3: *1 sc (*UK dc*) in next 3 sts, 2 sc (*UK dc*) in next st; rep from * to end (15 sts).

Rounds 4–6: 1 sc (*UK dc*) in each st to end.

Round 7: *1 sc (*UK dc*) in next 3 sts, dec over next 2 sts; rep from * to end (12 sts).

Round 8: *Dec over next 2 sts; rep from * to end (6 sts).

Tie off with a sl st, and leave enough yarn to sew the legs to the body.

Feet (x2)

Use dark gold yarn.

Work Rounds 1–5 as for arms.

Round 6: *1 sc (*UK dc*) in next st, dec over next 2 sts; rep from * to end (6 sts).

Tie off with a sl st, and close the feet. Leave enough yarn to sew the feet to the legs.

Tail

Use yellow acrylic yarn.

Round 1: 6 sc (*UK dc*) in magic ring (6 sts).

Round 2: 1 sc (*UK dc*) in each st to end.

Round 3: 2 sc (*UK dc*) in each st to end (12 sts).

Rounds 4 and 5: As Round 2.

Round 6: *1 sc (*UK dc*) in next st, 2 sc (*UK dc*) in next st; rep from * to end (18 sts).

Round 7: As Round 2.

Switch to red acrylic yarn.

Round 8: As Round 2.

Round 9: *1 sc (*UK dc*) in next 2 sts, 2 sc (*UK dc*) in next st; rep from * to end (24 sts).

Switch to yellow acrylic yarn.

Rounds 10 and 11: As Round 2.

Round 12: *1 sc (*UK dc*) in next 3 sts, 2 sc (*UK dc*) in next st; rep from * to end (30 sts).

Rounds 13–16: As Round 2.

Round 17: *1 sc (*UK dc*) in next 3 sts, dec over next 2 sts; rep from * to end (24 sts).

Round 18: As Round 2.

Switch to red acrylic yarn.

Round 19: As Round 2.

Round 20: *1 sc (*UK dc*) in next 2 sts, dec over next 2 sts; rep from * to end (18 sts).

Switch to yellow acrylic yarn.

Rounds 21 and 22: As Round 2.

Fill the tail and keep filling until the last round.

Round 23: *1 sc (*UK dc*) in next st, dec over next 2 sts; rep from * to end (12 sts).

Rounds 24 and 25: As Round 2.

Round 26: *Dec over next 2 sts; rep from * to end (6 sts).

Tie off with a sl st, and leave enough yarn to sew the tail to the body. Brush the tail to make it fluffy.

Ears (x2)

Use light yellow yarn.

Work Rounds 1 and 2 as for tail.

Round 3: *1 sc (*UK dc*) in next st, 2 sc (*UK dc*) in next st; rep from * to end (9 sts).

Round 4: As Round 2.

Round 5: *1 sc (*UK dc*) in next 2 sts, 2 sc (*UK dc*) in next st; rep from * to end (12 sts).

Switch to dark gold yarn.

Round 6: As Round 2.

Round 7: *1 sc (*UK dc*) in next 3 sts, 2 sc (*UK dc*) in next st; rep from * to end (15 sts).

Round 8: As Round 2.

Round 9: *1 sc (*UK dc*) in next 4 sts, 2 sc (*UK dc*) in next st; rep from * to end (18 sts).

Round 10: As Round 2.

Tie off with a sl st, and leave enough yarn to sew the ears to the head.

Snout

Use light yellow yarn.

Work Rounds 1 and 2 as for head/body.

Round 3: 1 sc (*UK dc*) in each st to end.

Round 4: *1 sc (*UK dc*) in next st, 2 sc (*UK dc*) in next st; rep from * to end (18 sts).

Fill the snout. Tie off with a sl st, and leave enough yarn to sew the snout to the head.

Whiskers (x2)

Use dark gold yarn. Turn work at the end of each row.

Row 1: 4 ch + 1 tch.

Row 2: Skip tch, 1 dc (*UK tr*) in next 4 ch, 4 ch + 1 tch.

Row 3: Skip tch, 1 dc (*UK tr*) in next 4 ch. Leave remaining sts unworked.

Tie off, and leave enough yarn to sew the whiskers to the head.

Putting all the parts together

Sew the belly to the body, approximately 3 rounds below the neck.

Sew the arms to the body, approximately 2 rounds below the neck.

Sew the feet to the legs, and then sew the legs to the body, approximately 7 rounds below the neck.

Sew the tail to the body, approximately 9 rounds below the neck.

Sew the ears to the head, at approximately Round 6.

Sew the snout to the head, at approximately Round 13.

Sew the whiskers to the head, at approximately Round 15.

Face

Cut 2 eyes out of white and black felt and paste these onto the head, at approximately Round 10, with 6 stitches between the eyes.

Cut a nose out of brown felt and paste it onto the snout at the top of Round 1.

Pinsnip

Materials:

4-ply (fine/sport weight) cotton yarn
light pink, 1 x 50g (1³/₄oz) ball
purple, 1 x 50g (1³/₄oz) ball
light purple, 1 x 50g (1³/₄oz) ball
Crochet cotton thread, black
Stuffing (fiberfill)
Black and white felt

Tools:

2.5mm (UK 13/US B-1) crochet hook
Tapestry (blunt-end) needle

Templates:

Eyes

Black   White

Difficulty

The making of the legs
and antennae can be a
bit fiddly because they
are quite small. For the
shell you sometimes
need to crochet in the
front loops only.

Instructions:

Unless stated otherwise, all sections/body parts begin
with a magic ring (see page 16 for instructions); the first
round should be worked into the ring.

Head/body

Use light pink yarn.

Round 1: 6 sc (*UK dc*) in magic ring (6 sts).

Round 2: 2 sc (*UK dc*) in each st to end (12 sts).

Round 3: *1 sc (*UK dc*) in next st, 2 sc (*UK dc*) in next st;
rep from * to end (18 sts).

Round 4: *1 sc (*UK dc*) in next 2 sts, 2 sc (*UK dc*) in next
st; rep from * to end (24 sts).

Round 5: *1 sc (*UK dc*) in next 3 sts, 2 sc (*UK dc*) in next
st; rep from * to end (30 sts).

Round 6: *1 sc (*UK dc*) in next 4 sts, 2 sc (*UK dc*) in next
st; rep from * to end (36 sts).

Round 7: *1 sc (*UK dc*) in next 5 sts, 2 sc (*UK dc*) in next
st; rep from * to end (42 sts).

Round 8: *1 sc (*UK dc*) in next 6 sts, 2 sc (*UK dc*) in next
st; rep from * to end (48 sts).

Round 9: *1 sc (*UK dc*) in next 7 sts, 2 sc (*UK dc*) in next
st; rep from * to end (54 sts).

Rounds 10–18: 1 sc (*UK dc*) in each st to end.

Round 19: *1 sc (*UK dc*) in next 7 sts, dec over next 2
sts; rep from * to end (48 sts).

Round 20: *1 sc (*UK dc*) in next 6 sts, dec over next 2
sts; rep from * to end (42 sts).

Round 21: *1 sc (*UK dc*) in next 5 sts, dec over next 2
sts; rep from * to end (36 sts).

Round 22: *1 sc (*UK dc*) in next 4 sts, dec over next 2
sts; rep from * to end (30 sts).

Round 23: *1 sc (*UK dc*) in next 3 sts, dec over next 2
sts; rep from * to end (24 sts).

Round 24: *1 sc (*UK dc*) in next 2 sts, dec over next 2
sts; rep from * to end (18 sts).

Fill the head/body and keep filling until the last round.

Round 25: *1 sc (*UK dc*) in next st, dec over next 2 sts; rep from * to end (12 sts).

Round 26: *Dec over next 2 sts; rep from * to end (6 sts).

Embroider the mouth (see opposite). Tie off with a sl st and close the head/body.

Legs (x6)

Use light pink yarn.

Round 1: 6 sc (*UK dc*) in magic ring (6 sts).

Rounds 2–5: 1 sc (*UK dc*) in each st to end.

Tie off with a sl st, and leave enough yarn to sew the legs to the head/body.

Antennae (x2)

Use light pink yarn.

Round 1: 6 sc (*UK dc*) in magic ring (6 sts).

Rounds 2–7: 1 sc (*UK dc*) in each st to end.

Tie off with a sl st, and leave enough yarn to sew the antennae to the head/body.

Claws ››› Part I (x2)

Use light pink yarn.

Work Rounds 1 and 2 as for legs.

Round 3: *1 sc (*UK dc*) in next st, 2 sc (*UK dc*) in next st; rep from * to end (9 sts).

Round 4: As Round 2.

Tie off with a sl st.

Claws ››› Part II (x2)

Use light pink yarn.

Work Rounds 1 and 2 as for legs.

Round 3: Holding Part I of claw next to Part II, work 1 sc (*UK dc*) in each st around Part II then each st around Part I to join (15 sts).

Round 4: As Round 2.

Round 5: *1 sc (*UK dc*) in next 3 sts, dec over next 2 sts; rep from * to end (12 sts).

Round 6: *1 sc (*UK dc*) in next 2 sts, dec over next 2 sts; rep from * to end (9 sts).

Round 7: *1 sc (*UK dc*) in next st, dec over next 2 sts; rep from * to end (6 sts).

Fill the claws. Tie off with a sl st, and leave enough yarn to sew the claws to the head/body.

Shell

Use purple yarn.

Note: *Rounds 8, 14, 20 and 26 should be worked in front loops only (FLO).*

Work Rounds 1 and 2 as for antennae.

Round 3: 2 sc (*UK dc*) in each st to end (12 sts).

Round 4: As Round 2.

Round 5: *1 sc (*UK dc*) in next st, 2 sc (*UK dc*) in next st; rep from * to end (18 sts).

Round 6: As Round 2.

Round 7: *1 sc (*UK dc*) in next 4 sts, dec over next 2 sts; rep from * to end (15 sts).

Switch to light purple yarn.

Round 8: FLO *1 sc (*UK dc*) in next 4 sts, 2 sc (*UK dc*) in next st; rep from * to end (18 sts).

Round 9: *1 sc (*UK dc*) in next 2 sts, 2 sc (*UK dc*) in next st; rep from * to end (24 sts).

Round 10: *1 sc (*UK dc*) in next 3 sts, 2 sc (*UK dc*) in next st; rep from * to end (30 sts).

Rounds 11 and 12: As Round 2.

Round 13: *1 sc (*UK dc*) in next 8 sts, dec over next 2 sts; rep from * to end (27 sts).

Switch to purple yarn.

Round 14: FLO *1 sc (*UK dc*) in next 8 sts, 2 sc (*UK dc*) in next st; rep from * to end (30 sts).

Round 15: *1 sc (*UK dc*) in next 4 sts, 2 sc (*UK dc*) in next st; rep from * to end (36 sts).

Round 16: *1 sc (*UK dc*) in next 5 sts, 2 sc (*UK dc*) in next st; rep from * to end (42 sts).

Rounds 17 and 18: As Round 2.

Round 19: *1 sc (*UK dc*) in next 12 sts, dec over next 2 sts; rep from * to end (39 sts).

Switch to light purple yarn.

Round 20: FLO *1 sc (*UK dc*) in next 12 sts, 2 sc (*UK dc*) in next st; rep from * to end (42 sts).

Round 21: *1 sc (*UK dc*) in next 6 sts, 2 sc (*UK dc*) in next st; rep from * to end (48 sts).

Round 22: *1 sc (*UK dc*) in next 7 sts, 2 sc (*UK dc*) in next st; rep from * to end (54 sts).

Rounds 23 and 24: As Round 2.

Round 25: *1 sc (*UK dc*) in next 7 sts, dec over next 2 sts; rep from * to end (48 sts).

Switch to purple yarn.

Round 26: FLO *1 sc (*UK dc*) in next 3 sts, 2 sc (*UK dc*) in next st; rep from * to end (60 sts).

Fill the shell. Tie off with a sl st, and leave enough yarn to sew the shell to the head/body.

Putting all the parts together

Sew 3 legs on both sides of the body, at approximately Round 20.

Sew the claws to the head/body, at approximately Round 18.

Sew the antennae to the head/body, at approximately Round 9.

Sew the shell askew to the top of the head/body.

Face

Cut 2 eyes out of black and white felt and paste these onto the head/body, somewhere at Round 11, with 4 stitches between the eyes.

Embroider a mouth on the head/body with black crochet cotton thread, somewhere at Round 17. Make sure you do this before you close up the head.

Cinzouri

What you need:

Materials:

4-ply (fine/sport weight) cotton yarn
    light grey, 1 x 50g (1³/₄oz) ball
    dark grey, 1 x 50g (1³/₄oz) ball
Stuffing (fiberfill)
Black and white felt

Tools:

2.5mm (UK 13/US B-1) crochet hook
Tapestry (blunt-end) needle

Templates:

Eyes

White

White

Black

Nose

Black

Difficulty

🐍 🐍 🐍 🐍 🐍

Although there are no difficult stitches, the spikes can be challenging to make. Also, for the head and legs, it is important to follow the instructions for increase and decrease in specific stitches.

Instructions:

Unless stated otherwise, all sections/body parts begin with a magic ring (see page 16 for instructions); the first round should be worked into the ring.

Head

Use light grey yarn.

Round 1: 6 sc (*UK dc*) in magic ring (6 sts).

Round 2: 2 sc (*UK dc*) in each st to end (12 sts).

Round 3: *1 sc (*UK dc*) in next st, 2 sc (*UK dc*) in next st; rep from * to end (18 sts).

Round 4: *1 sc (*UK dc*) in next 2 sts, 2 sc (*UK dc*) in next st; rep from * to end (24 sts).

Round 5: *1 sc (*UK dc*) in next 3 sts, 2 sc (*UK dc*) in next st; rep from * to end (30 sts).

Round 6: *1 sc (*UK dc*) in next 4 sts, 2 sc (*UK dc*) in next st; rep from * to end (36 sts).

Round 7: *1 sc (*UK dc*) in next 5 sts, 2 sc (*UK dc*) in next st; rep from * to end (42 sts).

Round 8: *1 sc (*UK dc*) in next 6 sts, 2 sc (*UK dc*) in next st; rep from * to end (48 sts).

Rounds 9–14: 1 sc (*UK dc*) in each st to end.

Round 15: 1 sc (*UK dc*) in next 17 sts, *2 sc (*UK dc*) in next st, 1 sc (*UK dc*) in next 2 sts; rep from * five more times, 1 sc (*UK dc*) in each st to end (54 sts).

Round 16: 1 sc (*UK dc*) in next 18 sts, *2 sc (*UK dc*) in next st, 1 sc (*UK dc*) in next 3 sts; rep from * five more times, 1 sc (*UK dc*) in each st to end (60 sts).

Rounds 17–19: As Round 14.

Round 20: 1 sc (*UK dc*) in next 18 sts, *dec over next 2 sts, 1 sc (*UK dc*) in next 3 sts; rep from * five more times, 1 sc (*UK dc*) in each st to end (54 sts).

Round 21: 1 sc (*UK dc*) in next 17 sts, *dec over next 2 sts, 1 sc (UK dc) in next 2 sts; rep from * five more times, 1 sc (*UK dc*) in each st to end (48 sts).

Round 22: *1 sc (*UK dc*) in next 6 sts, dec over next 2 sts; rep from * to end (42 sts).

Round 23: *1 sc (*UK dc*) in next 5 sts, dec over next 2 sts; rep from * to end (36 sts).

Round 24: *1 sc (*UK dc*) in next 4 sts, dec over next 2 sts; rep from * to end (30 sts).

Round 25: *1 sc (*UK dc*) in next 3 sts, dec over next 2 sts; rep from * to end (24 sts).

Round 26: *1 sc (*UK dc*) in next 2 sts, dec over next 2 sts; rep from * to end (18 sts).

Fill the head. Tie off with a sl st, and leave enough yarn to sew the head to the body.

Body

Use light grey yarn.

Work Rounds 1–4 as for head.

Rounds 5–15: 1 sc (*UK dc*) in each st to end.

Round 16: *1 sc (*UK dc*) in next 2 sts, dec over next 2 sts; rep from * to end (18 sts).

Fill the body and keep filling until the last round.

Round 17: *1 sc (*UK dc*) in next st, dec over next 2 sts; rep from * to end (12 sts).

Round 18: *Dec over next 2 sts; rep from * to end (6 sts).

Tie off with a sl st and close the body.

Tail

Use light grey yarn.

Round 1: 6 sc (*UK dc*) in magic ring (6 sts).

Round 2: 1 sc (*UK dc*) in each st to end.

Round 3: *1 sc (*UK dc*) in next st, 2 sc (*UK dc*) in next st; rep from * to end (9 sts).

Rounds 4 and 5: As Round 2.

Round 6: *1 sc (*UK dc*) in next 2 sts, 2 sc (*UK dc*) in next st; rep from * to end (12 sts).

Round 7: As Round 2.

Fill the tail. Tie off with a sl st, and leave enough yarn to sew the tail to the body.

Spines ››› Part I

Use dark grey yarn.

Row 1: 20 ch + 1 tch.

Row 2: Turn work, skip tch, *1 sl st in next ch, work 3 ch + 1 tch, turn work, skip tch, 1 sl st in next ch of 3-ch, 1 sc (*UK dc*) in next 2 ch of 3-ch, 1 sl st in next ch of original chain; rep from * nine more times, until you have 10 rounded points and all ch have been worked.

Tie off, and leave enough yarn to sew the spine strip to the body.

Spines ››› Part II

Use dark grey yarn.

Row 1: 22 ch + 1 tch.

Row 2: Work as for Row 2 of Part I, repeating from * until you have 11 rounded points and all ch have been worked.

Tie off, and leave enough yarn to sew the spine strip to the body.

Spines ››› Part III

Use dark grey yarn.

Row 1: 24 ch + tch.

Row 2: Work as for Row 2 of Part I, repeating from * until you have 12 rounded points and all ch have been worked.

Tie off, and leave enough yarn to sew the spine strip to the body.

Spines ››› Part IV

Use dark grey yarn.

Row 1: 26 ch + 1 tch.

Row 2: Work as for Row 2 of Part I, repeating from * until you have 13 rounded points and all ch have been worked.

Tie off, and leave enough yarn to sew the spine strip to the body.

Feet (x4)

Use light grey yarn.

Round 1: 8 sc (*UK dc*) in magic ring (8 sts).

Round 2: *2 sc (*UK dc*) in each of next 2 sts, 1 sc (*UK dc*) in next 2 sts; rep from * to end (12 sts).

Round 3: 1 sc (*UK dc*) in each st to end.

Round 4: [Dec over next 2 sts] twice, 1 sc (*UK dc*) in each st to end (10 sts).

Round 5: *1 sc (*UK dc*) in next 3 sts, dec over next 2 sts; rep from * to end (8 sts).

Fill the feet. Tie off with a sl st, and leave enough yarn to sew the feet to the body.

Outer ears (x2)

Use light grey yarn.

Work Rounds 1–3 as for head.

Rounds 4–7: 1 sc (*UK dc*) in each st to end.

Tie off with a sl st, and leave enough yarn to sew the ears to the head.

Inner ears (x2)

Use dark grey yarn.

Round 1: 6 sc (*UK dc*) in magic ring (6 sts).

Tie off with a sl st, and leave enough yarn to sew this part to the outer ears.

Tuft bottom

Use dark grey yarn.

Round 1: 12 ch, sl st in 1st ch made to join the round.

Round 2: *1 sl st in next ch, work 3 ch + 1 tch, turn work, skip tch, 1 sl st in next ch of 3-ch, 1 sc (*UK dc*) in next 2 ch of 3-ch, sl st in next ch of original chain; rep from * five more times until you have 6 round bobbles in a flower-like shape.

Tie off and leave enough yarn to sew the tuft to the top of head.

Tuft top

Use dark grey yarn.

Round 1: 6 sc (*UK dc*) in magic ring. (6 sts).

Round 2: *1 sl st in next st, work 3 ch + 1 tch, turn work, skip tch, 1 sl st in next ch of 3-ch, 1 sc (*UK dc*) in next 2 ch of 3-ch, 1 sl st in next st; rep from * two more times until you have 3 bobbles in a three-leaved, clover-like shape.

Tie off, and leave enough yarn to sew the tuft top to the top of head.

Putting all the parts together

Sew the head to the body, at approximately Round 5.

Sew the tail to the back of the body.

Sew the feet to the body – the forelegs at approximately Round 5, and the hind legs at Round 13.

Sew the spines to the back of the body, starting just beneath the head.

Sew the inner ears into the outer ears; and then sew the ears to the head, at approximately Round 6.

Sew the tuft bottom to the top of the head then sew tuft top in centre of tuft bottom.

Face

Cut 2 eyes out of white and black felt and paste these onto the head, at approximately Round 10.

Cut a nose out of black felt and paste it onto the head, at approximately Round 17.

55

Kajuku

Materials:

4-ply (fine/sport weight) cotton yarn
  green, 1 x 50g (1³/₄oz) ball
  brown, 1 x 50g (1³/₄oz) ball
  yellow, small amount
  dark green, 1 x 50g (1³/₄oz) ball
Stuffing (fiberfill)
White, brown and black felt

Tools:

2.5mm (UK 13/US B-1) crochet hook
Tapestry (blunt-end) needle

Templates:

Eyes

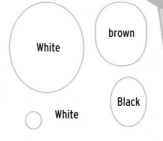

White

brown

White

Black

Difficulty

🐾 🐾 🐾 🐾 🐾

No difficult stitches. The making of the feet can be a bit fiddly because they are quite small.

Instructions:

Unless stated otherwise, all sections/body parts begin with a magic ring (see page 16 for instructions); the first round should be worked into the ring.

Head/body

Use green yarn.

Round 1: 6 sc (*UK dc*) in magic ring (6 sts).

Round 2: 2 sc (*UK dc*) in each st to end (12 sts).

Round 3: *1 sc (*UK dc*) in next st, 2 sc (*UK dc*) in next st; rep from * to end (18 sts).

Round 4: *1 sc (*UK dc*) in next 2 sts, 2 sc (*UK dc*) in next st; rep from * to end (24 sts).

Round 5: *1 sc (*UK dc*) in next 3 sts, 2 sc (*UK dc*) in next st; rep from * to end (30 sts).

Round 6: *1 sc (*UK dc*) in next 4 sts, 2 sc (*UK dc*) in next st; rep from * to end (36 sts).

Round 7: *1 sc (*UK dc*) in next 5 sts, 2 sc (*UK dc*) in next st; rep from * to end (42 sts).

Round 8: 1 sc (*UK dc*) in each st to end.

Round 9: *1 sc (*UK dc*) in next 6 sts, 2 sc (*UK dc*) in next st; rep from * to end (48 sts).

Rounds 10 and 11: As Round 8.

Round 12: *1 sc (*UK dc*) in next 7 sts, 2 sc (*UK dc*) in next st; rep from * to end (54 sts).

Rounds 13–17: As Round 8.

Switch to brown yarn.

Round 18: As Round 8.

Round 19: *1 sc (*UK dc*) in next 7 sts, dec over next 2 sts; rep from * to end (48 sts).

Round 20: As Round 8.

Round 21: *1 sc *UK dc*) in next 6 sts, dec over next 2 sts; rep from * to end (42 sts).

Round 22: As Round 8.

57

Round 23: *1 sc (*UK dc*) in next 5 sts, dec over next 2 sts; rep from * to end (36 sts).

Round 24: *1 sc (*UK dc*) in next 4 sts, dec over next 2 sts; rep from * to end (30 sts).

Round 25: *1 sc (*UK dc*) in next 3 sts, dec over next 2 sts; rep from * to end (24 sts).

Round 26: *1 sc (*UK dc*) in next 2 sts, dec over next 2 sts; rep from * to end (18 sts).

Fill the head/body and keep filling until the last round.

Round 27: *1 sc (*UK dc*) in next st, dec over next 2 sts; rep from * to end (12 sts).

Round 28: *Dec over next 2 sts; rep from * to end (6 sts).

Tie off with a sl st and close the head/body.

Wings (x2)

Use green yarn.

Work Rounds 1–3 as for head/body.

Rounds 4–7: 1 sc (*UK dc*) in each st to end.

Tie off with a sl st, and leave enough yarn to sew the wings to the head/body.

Feet ››› Part I (x2)

Use yellow yarn.

Round 1: 6 sc (*UK dc*) in magic ring (6 sts).

Rounds 2 and 3: 1 sc (*UK dc*) in each st to end.

Tie off with a sl st.

Feet ››› Part II (x2)

Use yellow yarn.

Work Rounds 1–3 as for Part I of feet.

Round 4: Holding Part I of feet next to Part II, work 1 sc (*UK dc*) in each st around Part II then each st around Part I to join (12 sts).

Round 5: *1 sc (*UK dc*) in next 2 sts, dec over next 2 sts; rep from * to end (9 sts).

Round 6: As Round 3.

Round 7: *1 sc (*UK dc*) in next st, dec over next 2 sts; rep from * to end (6 sts).

Tie off with a sl st and close the feet. Leave enough yarn to sew the feet to the head/body.

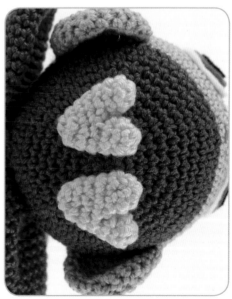

Beak

Use yellow yarn.

Round 1: 6 sc (*UK dc*) in magic ring (6 sts).

Round 2: 1 sc (*UK dc*) in each st to end.

Round 3: *1 sc (*UK dc*) in next st, 2 sc (*UK dc*) in next st; rep from * to end (9 sts).

Round 4: As Round 2.

Round 5: *1 sc (*UK dc*) in next 2 sts, 2 sc (*UK dc*) in next st; rep from * to end (12 sts).

Fill the beak. Tie off with a sl st, and leave enough yarn to sew the beak to the head/body.

Tail

Use dark green yarn.

Work Rounds 1 and 2 as for head/body.

Rounds 3 and 4: 1 sc (*UK dc*) in each st to end.

Tie off with a sl st, and leave enough yarn to sew the tail to the head/body.

Leaves (x5)

Use dark green yarn.

Work Rounds 1–5 as for beak.

Round 6: As Round 2.

Round 7: *1 sc (*UK dc*) in next 3 sts, 2 sc (*UK dc*) in next st; rep from * to end (15 sts).

Round 8: As Round 2.

Round 9: *1 sc (*UK dc*) in next 4 sts, 2 sc (*UK dc*) in next st; rep from * to end (18 sts).

Round 10: As Round 2.

Round 11: *1 sc (*UK dc*) in next 5 sts, 2 sc (*UK dc*) in next st; rep from * to end (21 sts).

Rounds 12–15: As Round 2.

Round 16: *1 sc (*UK dc*) in next 5 sts, dec over next 2 sts; rep from * to end (18 sts).

Round 17: As Round 2.

Round 18: *1 sc (*UK dc*) in next st, dec over next 2 sts; rep from * to end (12 sts).

Round 19: As Round 2.

Round 20: *1 sc (*UK dc*) in next 2 sts, dec over next 2 sts; rep from * to end (9 sts).

Tie off with a sl st, and leave enough yarn to sew the leaves to the tail.

Putting all the parts together

Sew the wings to the head/body, at approximately Round 17.

Sew the feet to the bottom of the body.

Sew the beak to the head/body, at approximately Round 13.

Sew the tail to the head/body, at approximately Round 16.

Sew 3 leaves to Round 4 of the tail and 2 leaves to Round 3. Sew the leaves to the head/body too to keep them close together.

Face

Cut 2 eyes out of white, brown and black felt and paste these onto the head/body, at approximately Round 9, with 5 stitches between the eyes.

Oscur

Materials:

4-ply (fine/sport weight) cotton yarn
  black, 1 x 50g (1³/₄oz) ball
  light purple, 1 x 50g (1³/₄oz) ball
Stuffing (fiberfill)
Black, white and red felt

Tools:

2.5mm (UK 13/US B-1) crochet hook
Tapestry (blunt-end) needle

Templates:

Eyes

Red

Black

White

Difficulty

No difficult stitches.
To get the shape of the
feet, it is important to
follow the instructions for
increase and decrease in
specific stitches.

Instructions:

Unless stated otherwise, all sections/body parts begin with a magic ring (see page 16 for instructions); the first round should be worked into the ring.

Head/body

Use black yarn.

Round 1: 6 sc (*UK dc*) in magic ring (6 sts).

Round 2: 2 sc (*UK dc*) in each st to end (12 sts).

Round 3: *1 sc (*UK dc*) in next st, 2 sc (*UK dc*) in next st; rep from * to end (18 sts).

Round 4: *1 sc (*UK dc*) in next 2 sts, 2 sc (*UK dc*) in next st; rep from * to end (24 sts).

Round 5: *1 sc (*UK dc*) in next 3 sts, 2 sc (*UK dc*) in next st; rep from * to end (30 sts).

Round 6: *1 sc (*UK dc*) in next 4 sts, 2 sc (*UK dc*) in next st; rep from * to end (36 sts).

Round 7: *1 sc (*UK dc*) in next 5 sts, 2 sc (*UK dc*) in next st; rep from * to end (42 sts).

Round 8: *1 sc (*UK dc*) in next 6 sts, 2 sc (*UK dc*) in next st; rep from * to end (48 sts).

Rounds 9–16: 1 sc (*UK dc*) in each st to end.

Round 17: *1 sc (*UK dc*) in next 6 sts, dec over next 2 sts; rep from * to end (42 sts).

Round 18: *1 sc (*UK dc*) in next 5 sts, dec over next 2 sts; rep from * to end (36 sts).

Round 19: *1 sc (*UK dc*) in next 4 sts, dec over next 2 sts; rep from * to end (30 sts).

Round 20: *1 sc (*UK dc*) in next 3 sts, dec over next 2 sts; rep from * to end (24 sts).

Round 21: *1 sc (*UK dc*) in next 2 sts, dec over next 2 sts; rep from * to end (18 sts).

Fill the head/body, and keep filling until the last round.

Rounds 22 and 23: As Rounds 4 and 5 (30 sts).

Rounds 24–28: As Round 16.

Rounds 29 and 30: As Rounds 20 and 21 (18 sts).

Round 31: *1 sc (*UK dc*) in next st, dec over next 2 sts; rep from * to end (12 sts).

Round 32: *Dec over next 2 sts; rep from * to end (6 sts).

Tie off with a sl st and close the head/body.

Feet (x2)

Use black yarn.

Round 1: 8 sc (*UK dc*) in magic ring (8 sts).

Round 2: *2 sc (*UK dc*) in each of next 2 sts, 1 sc (*UK dc*) in next 2 sts; rep from * to end (12 sts).

Round 3: 1 sc (*UK dc*) in each st to end.

Round 4: [Dec over next 2 sts] twice, 1 sc (*UK dc*) in each st to end (10 sts).

Round 5: *1 sc (*UK dc*) in next 3 sts, dec over next 2 sts; rep from * to end (8 sts).

Tie off with a sl st, and leave enough yarn to sew the feet to the body.

Hood (main)

Use light purple yarn.

Work Rounds 1–8 as for head/body.

Rounds 9–12: 1 sc (*UK dc*) in each st to end.

Round 13: 1 sc (*UK dc*) in each st to end, turn.

Row 14: 1 tch, 1 sc (*UK dc*) in next 42 sts and turn, leaving remaining sts unworked (42 sts). Continue on these sts only.

Row 15: 1 tch, dec over next 2 sts, 1 sc (*UK dc*) in each st to last 2 sts, dec over last 2 sts, turn (40 sts).

Row 16: 1 tch, 1 sc (*UK dc*) in each st to end, turn.

Rows 17 and 18: As Rows 15 and 16 (38 sts).

Tie off with a sl st.

Hood (pointed top)

Use light purple yarn.

Round 1: 6 sc (*UK dc*) in magic ring (6 sts).

Round 2: 1 sc (*UK dc*) in each st to end.

Round 3: *1 sc (*UK dc*) in next st, 2 sc (*UK dc*) in next st; rep from * to end (9 sts).

Rounds 4 and 5: As Round 2.

Round 6: *1 sc (*UK dc*) in next 2 sts, 2 sc (*UK dc*) in next st; rep from * to end (12 sts).

Round 7: As Round 3 (18 sts).

Round 8: As Round 6 (24 sts).

Rounds 9 and 10: As Round 2.

Round 11: *1 sc (*UK dc*) in next 2 sts, dec over next 2 sts; rep from * to end (18 sts).

Round 12: As Round 6 (24 sts).

Round 13: *1 sc (*UK dc*) in next 3 sts, 2 sc (*UK dc*) in next st; rep from * to end (30 sts).

Round 14: *1 sc (*UK dc*) in next 4 sts, 2 sc (*UK dc*) in next st; rep from * to end (36 sts).

Rounds 15 and 16: As Round 2.

Fill the top. Tie off with a sl st, and leave enough yarn to sew the top to the hood.

Cape

Use light purple yarn. After each row turn work. Leave enough yarn at the beginning to sew the cape to the hood.

Row 1: 18 ch + 1 tch.

Row 2: Skip tch, 2 sc (*UK dc*) in next ch, 1 sc (*UK dc*) in each ch to last ch, 2 sc (*UK dc*) in last ch (20 sts).

Row 3: 1 tch, 1 sc (*UK dc*) in each st to last st, 2 sc (*UK dc*) in last st (21 sts).

Rows 4–11: Repeat Row 3 eight more times (29 sts).

Tie off.

Cape ties (x2)

Use light purple yarn.

Row 1: 14 ch + 1 tch.

Row 2: Turn work, skip tch, 1 sl st in each ch to end (14 sts).

Tie off, and leave enough yarn to sew the ties to the cape.

Putting all the parts together

Sew the feet to the bottom of the body.

Sew the pointed to to the hood.

Sew the cape to the bottom of the hood.

Sew the cape ties to the cape.

Place the hood on the head and then tie the cape ties around neck.

Face

Cut 2 eyes out of red, black and white felt and paste these onto the head, at approximately Round 10, with 4 stitches between the eyes.

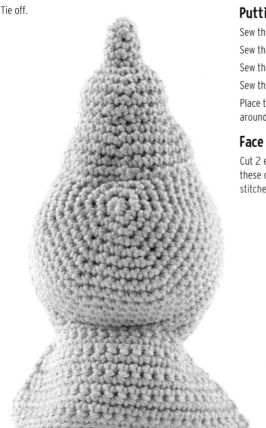

Mon-Chi

Materials:

4-ply (fine/sport weight) cotton yarn
camel brown, 1 x 50g (1³/₄oz) ball
off white, 1 x 50g (1³/₄oz) ball
yellow, small amount
green, small amount
blue, small amount
Stuffing (fiberfill)
Jewellery wire, 1mm (18 gauge) thick
Black and white felt

Tools:

2.5mm (UK 13/US B-1) crochet hook
Tapestry (blunt-end) needle

Templates:

Eyes

Black

White

Difficulty

It is important to follow the instructions carefully here, especially for the head and paint splashes.

Instructions:

Unless stated otherwise, all sections/body parts begin with a magic ring (see page 16 for instructions); the first round should be worked into the ring.

Head/body

Use camel brown yarn.

Round 1: 6 sc (*UK dc*) in magic ring (6 sts).

Round 2: 2 sc (*UK dc*) in each st to end (12 sts).

Round 3: *1 sc (*UK dc*) in next st, 2 sc (*UK dc*) in next st; rep from * to end (18 sts).

Round 4: *1 sc (*UK dc*) in next 2 sts, 2 sc (*UK dc*) in next st; rep from * to end (24 sts).

Round 5: *1 sc (*UK dc*) in next 3 sts, 2 sc (*UK dc*) in next st; rep from * to end (30 sts).

Round 6: *1 sc (*UK dc*) in next 4 sts, 2 sc (*UK dc*) in next st; rep from * to end (36 sts).

Round 7: *1 sc (*UK dc*) in next 5 sts, 2 sc (*UK dc*) in next st; rep from * to end (42 sts).

Round 8: *1 sc (*UK dc*) in next 6 sts, 2 sc (*UK dc*) in next st; rep from * to end (48 sts).

Rounds 9–15: 1 sc (*UK dc*) in each st to end.

Round 16: *1 sc (*UK dc*) in next 6 sts, dec over next 2 sts; rep from * to end (42 sts).

Round 17: *1 sc (*UK dc*) in next 5 sts, dec over next 2 sts; rep from * to end (36 sts).

Round 18: *1 sc (*UK dc*) in next 4 sts, dec over next 2 sts; rep from * to end (30 sts).

Round 19: *1 sc (*UK dc*) in next 3 sts, dec over next 2 sts; rep from * to end (24 sts).

Round 20: *1 sc (*UK dc*) in next 2 sts, dec over next 2 sts; rep from * to end (18 sts).

Fill the head/body and keep filling until the last round.

Rounds 21 and 22: As Rounds 4 and 5 (30 sts).

Rounds 23–28: As Round 15.

Rounds 29 and 30: As Rounds 19 and 20 (18 sts).

Round 31: *1 sc (*UK dc*) in next st, dec over next 2 sts; rep from * to end (12 sts).

Round 32: *Dec over next 2 sts; rep from * to end (6 sts).

Embroider the mouth (see opposite). Tie off with a sl st and close the head/body.

Face

Use off white yarn.

Work Rounds 1–5 as for head/body.

Round 6: 1 sc (*UK dc*) in next 5 sts, 1 dc (*UK tr*) in next 8 sts, 1 sc (*UK dc*) in next st, 1 sl st in next 2 sts, 1 sc (*UK dc*) in next st, 1 dc (*UK tr*) in next 8 sts, 1 sc (*UK dc*) in next 5 sts (30 sts).

Tie off with a sl st, and leave enough yarn to sew the face to the head.

Outer ear (x2)

Use camel brown yarn.

Work Rounds 1–4 as for head/body.

Rounds 5–7: 1 sc (*UK dc*) in each st to end.

Round 8: *1 sc (*UK dc*) in next 6 sts, dec over next 2 sts; rep from * to end (21 sts).

Tie off with a sl st, and leave enough yarn to sew the ears to the head.

Inner ear (x2)

Use green and yellow yarn, making 1 of each colour.

Round 1: 6 sc (*UK dc*) in magic ring, turn (6 sts).

Round 2: 1 tch, 1 sc (*UK dc*) in each st to end.

Tie off with a sl st, and leave enough yarn to sew this part to the outer ears.

Beret

Use off white yarn.

Round 1: 6 sc (*UK dc*) in magic ring (6 sts).

Rounds 2 and 3: 1 sc (*UK dc*) in each st to end.

Rounds 4–9: Work as Rounds 2–7 of head/body (42 sts).

Rounds 10 and 11: 1 sc (*UK dc*) in each st to end.

Round 12: *1 sc (*UK dc*) in next 5 sts, dec over next 2 sts; rep from * to end (36 sts).

Round 13: *1 sc (*UK dc*) in next 4 sts, dec over next 2 sts; rep from * to end (30 sts).

Tie off with a sl st, and leave enough yarn to sew the beret to the head.

Feet (x2)

Use camel brown yarn.

Round 1: 6 sc (*UK dc*) in magic ring (6 sts).

Round 2: *2 sc (*UK dc*) in each of next 2 sts, 1 sc (*UK dc*) in next st; rep from * to end (10 sts).

Round 3: Work 2 sc (*UK dc*) in 2nd, 3rd, 7th and 8th sts, working 1 sc (*UK dc*) in all other sts (14 sts).

Round 4: 1 sc (*UK dc*) in each st to end.

Round 5: 1 sc (*UK dc*) in next st, [dec over next 2 sts] twice, 1 sc (*UK dc*) in each st to end (12 sts).

Round 6: *1 sc (*UK dc*) in next 2 sts, dec over next 2 sts; rep from * to end (9 sts).

Rounds 7 and 8: As Round 4.

Fill the feet. Tie off with a sl st, and leave enough yarn to sew the feet to the body.

Arms (x2)

Use camel brown yarn.

Round 1: 6 sc (*UK dc*) in magic ring (6 sts).

Round 2: *1 sc (*UK dc*) in next 2 sts, 2 sc (*UK dc*) in next st; rep from * to end (8 sts).

Rounds 3–8: 1 sc (*UK dc*) in each st to end.

Fill the arms. Tie off with a sl st, and leave enough yarn to sew the arms to the body.

Tail

Use blue yarn.

Round 1: 6 sc (*UK dc*) in magic ring (6 sts).

Round 2: 1 sc (*UK dc*) in each st to end.

Round 3: *1 sc (*UK dc*) in next st, 2 sc (*UK dc*) in next st; rep from * to end (9 sts).

Round 4: As Round 2.

Round 5: 2 sc (*UK dc*) in each st to end (18 sts).

Round 6: 1 sc (*UK dc*) in each st to end, alternating between off white and blue yarn every 3 sts.

Continue with off white yarn only.

Rounds 7 and 8: As Round 2.

Round 9: *1 sc (*UK dc*) in next st, dec over next 2 sts; rep from * to end (12 sts).

Round 10: *Dec over next 2 sts; rep from * to end (6 sts).

Switch to camel brown yarn.

Fill the tail and keep filling until the last round.

Rounds 11–28: As Round 2.

Insert some jewellery wire into the tail and bend it into your chosen shape.

Tie off with a sl st, and leave enough yarn to sew the tail to the body.

Paint splashes (x6)

Use yellow, green and blue yarn, making 2 of each colour.

Round 1: 6 sc (*UK dc*) in magic ring (6 sts).

Round 2: *1 sl st in next st, work 1 ch + 1 tch, turn work, skip tch, 1 dc (*UK tr*) in 1-ch, 1 sl st in next st; rep from * to end.

Tie off, and leave enough yarn to sew the paint splashes to the body.

Putting all the parts together

Sew the face to the head, at approximately Round 8.

Sew the inner ears onto the outer ears and then sew the ears to the head, at approximately Round 10.

Sew the beret to the top of the head. Sew into the bobble in the middle of the hat to flatten it.

Sew the feet to the bottom of the body.

Sew the arms to the body, approximately 2 rounds below the neck.

Sew the tail to the body, approximately 8 rounds below the neck.

Sew the paint splashes to the body, using the photos to guide you.

Face

Cut 2 eyes out of black and white felt and paste these onto the face.

Embroider a mouth on the face with black yarn. Make sure you do this before you sew it onto the head.

Boink

Materials:

4-ply (fine/sport weight) cotton yarn
  orange, 1 x 50g (1³/₄oz) ball
  black, 1 x 50g (1³/₄oz) ball
  medium pink, small amount
Stuffing (fiberfill)
Jewellery wire, 1mm (18 gauge) thick
Black and white felt

Tools:

2.5mm (UK 13/US B-1) crochet hook
Tapestry (blunt-end) needle

Templates:

Eyes

Black

White   White

Nose

Black

Difficulty

To get the shape of the feet, it is important to follow the instructions for increase and decrease in specific stitches. For the stripes you need to know the (*UK htr*).

Instructions:

Unless stated otherwise, all sections/body parts begin with a magic ring (see page 16 for instructions); the first round should be worked into the ring.

Head/body

Use orange yarn.

Round 1: 6 sc (*UK dc*) in magic ring (6 sts).

Round 2: 2 sc (*UK dc*) in each st to end (12 sts).

Round 3: *1 sc (*UK dc*) in next st, 2 sc (*UK dc*) in next st; rep from * to end (18 sts).

Round 4: *1 sc (*UK dc*) in next 2 sts, 2 sc (*UK dc*) in next st; rep from * to end (24 sts).

Round 5: *1 sc (*UK dc*) in next 3 sts, 2 sc (*UK dc*) in next st; rep from * to end (30 sts).

Round 6: *1 sc (*UK dc*) in next 4 sts, 2 sc (*UK dc*) in next st; rep from * to end (36 sts).

Round 7: 1 sc (*UK dc*) in each st to end.

Round 8: *1 sc (*UK dc*) in next 5 sts, 2 sc (*UK dc*) in next st; rep from * to end (42 sts).

Rounds 9 and 10: As Round 7.

Round 11: *1 sc (*UK dc*) in next 6 sts, 2 sc (*UK dc*) in next st; rep from * to end (48 sts).

Rounds 12–17: As Round 7.

Round 18: *1 sc (*UK dc*) in next 6 sts, dec over next 2 sts; rep from * to end (42 sts).

Rounds 19 and 20: As Round 7.

Round 21: *1 sc (*UK dc*) in next 5 sts, dec over next 2 sts; rep from * to end (36 sts).

Round 22: As Round 7.

Round 23: *1 sc (*UK dc*) in next 4 sts, dec over next 2 sts; rep from * to end (30 sts).

Round 24: *1 sc (*UK dc*) in next 3 sts, dec over next 2 sts; rep from * to end (24 sts).

Round 25: *1 sc (*UK dc*) in next 2 sts, dec over next 2 sts; rep from * to end (18 sts).

Fill the head/body and keep filling until the last round.

Round 26: *1 sc (*UK dc*) in next st, dec over next 2 sts; rep from * to end (12 sts).

Round 27: *Dec over next 2 sts; rep from * to end (6 sts).

Embroider the mouth (see opposite). Tie off with a sl st and close the head/body.

Stripes (x4)

Use black yarn.

Row 1: 12 ch + 1 tch.

Row 2: Turn work, skip tch, 1 sl st in next 2 ch, 1 sc (*UK dc*) in next 2 ch, 1 hdc (*UK htr*) in next 4 ch, 1 sc (*UK dc*) in next 2 ch, 1 sl st in last 2 ch.

Tie off, and leave enough yarn to sew the stripes to the head/body.

Outer ears (x2)

Use orange yarn.

Work Rounds 1–5 as for head/body.

Rounds 6–10: 1 sc (*UK dc*) in each st to end.

Round 11: *1 sc (*UK dc*) in next 3 sts, dec over next 2 sts; rep from * to end (24 sts).

Round 12: *1 sc (*UK dc*) in next 2 sts, dec over next 2 sts; rep from * to end (18 sts).

Tie off with a sl st, and leave enough yarn to sew the ears to the head/body.

Inner ears (x2)

Use medium pink yarn.

Work Rounds 1–3 as for head/body.

Switch to black yarn.

Work Round 4 as for head/body.

Tie off with a sl st, and leave enough yarn to sew this part to the outer ears.

Arms (x2)

Use orange yarn.

Round 1: 6 sc (*UK dc*) in magic ring (6 sts).

Round 2: *1 sc (*UK dc*) in next 2 sts, 2 sc (*UK dc*) in next st; rep from * to end (8 sts).

Round 3: 1 sc (*UK dc*) in each st to end.

Round 4: *1 sc (*UK dc*) in next 3 sts, 2 sc (*UK dc*) in next st; rep from * to end (10 sts).

Fill the arms. Tie off with a sl st, and leave enough yarn to sew the arms to the head/body.

Feet (x2)

Use black yarn.

Round 1: 6 sc (*UK dc*) in magic ring (6 sts).

Round 2: 2 sc (*UK dc*) in each st to end (12 sts).

Round 3: *2 sc (*UK dc*) in each of next 3 sts, 1 sc (*UK dc*) in next 3 sts; rep from * to end (18 sts).

Round 4: 1 sc (*UK dc*) in each st to end.

Round 5: [Dec over next 2 sts] three times, 1 sc (*UK dc*) in each st to end (15 sts).

Round 6: *1 sc (*UK dc*) in next st, dec over next 2 sts; rep from * to end (10 sts).

Fill the feet. Tie off with a sl st, and leave enough yarn to sew the feet to the head/body.

Tail

Use black yarn.

Round 1: 6 sc (*UK dc*) in magic ring (6 sts).

Round 2: 1 sc (*UK dc*) in each st to end.

Round 3: *1 sc (*UK dc*) in next 2 sts, 2 sc (*UK dc* in next st; rep from * to end (8 sts).

Round 4: As Round 2.

Start filling and keep filling until the last round.

Switch to orange yarn.

Round 5–7: As Round 2.

Switch to black yarn.

Round 8–10: As Round 2.

Switch to orange yarn.

Round 11–13: As Round 2.

Switch to black yarn.

Continuing to switch colours every three rounds as set, repeat Rounds 8–13 four more times.

Insert some jewellery wire into the tail, and bend it into your chosen shape.

Tie off with a sl st, and leave enough yarn to sew the tail to the head/body.

Putting all the parts together

Sew the inner ears to the outer ears, then sew the ears to the head/body, at approximately Round 5.

Sew the arms to the head/body, at approximately Round 17.

Sew the feet to the bottom of the head/body.

Sew the tail to the head/body, at approximately Round 25.

Sew the 4 stripes to the head/body, with 2 on each side, at approximately Round 15 and 18.

Face

Cut 2 eyes out of black and white felt, and paste these onto the head/body at approximately Round 9, with 5 stitches between the eyes.

Cut a nose out of black felt and paste it onto the head/body, at approximately Round 14.

Embroider a mouth pn the head/body with black yarn, at approximately Round 16. Make sure you do this before you close up the head/body,

Glamastar

Difficulty
🐕 🐕 🐕 🐕 🐕

Only the tail can be a bit difficult, as it requires several stitches.

Materials:

4-ply (fine/sport weight) cotton yarn
   turquoise blue, 1 x 50g (1³/₄oz) ball
   green, 1 x 50g (1³/₄oz) ball
   black, small amount
   red, small amount
Stuffing (fiberfill)
Black, white and red felt

Tools:

2.5mm (UK 13/US B-1) crochet hook
Tapestry (blunt-end) needle

Templates:

Eyes

Black

White

Red

Instructions:

Unless stated otherwise, all sections/body parts begin with a magic ring (see page 16 for instructions); the first round should be worked into the ring.

Head/body

Use turquoise blue yarn.

Round 1: 6 sc (*UK dc*) in magic ring (6 sts).

Round 2: 2 sc (*UK dc*) in each st to end (12 sts).

Round 3: *1 sc (*UK dc*) in next st, 2 sc (*UK dc*) in next st; rep from * to end (18 sts).

Rounds 4 and 5: 1 sc (*UK dc*) in each st to end.

Round 6: *1 sc (*UK dc*) in next 2 sts, 2 sc (*UK dc*) in next st; rep from * to end (24 sts).

Rounds 7 and 8: As Round 5.

Round 9: *1 sc (*UK dc*) in next 3 sts, 2 sc (*UK dc*) in next st; rep from * to end (30 sts).

Round 10: As Round 5.

Round 11: *1 sc (*UK dc*) in next 4 sts, 2 sc (*UK dc*) in next st; rep from * to end (36 sts).

Round 12: *1 sc (*UK dc*) in next 5 sts, 2 sc (*UK dc*) in next st; rep from * to end (42 sts).

Round 13: *1 sc (*UK dc*) in next 6 sts, 2 sc (*UK dc*) in next st; rep from * to end (48 sts).

Rounds 14-21: As Round 5.

Round 22: *1 sc (*UK dc*) in next 6 sts, dec over next 2 sts; rep from * to end (42 sts).

Rounds 23 and 24: As Round 5.

Round 25: *1 sc (*UK dc*) in next 5 sts, dec over next 2 sts; rep from * to end (36 sts).

Rounds 26 and 27: As Round 5.

Round 28: *1 sc (*UK dc*) in next 4 sts, dec over next 2 sts; rep from * to end (30 sts).

Round 29: As Round 5.

Round 30: *1 sc (*UK dc*) in next 3 sts, dec over next 2 sts; rep from * to end (24 sts).

Round 31: As Round 5.

Round 32: *1 sc (*UK dc*) in next 2 sts, dec over next 2 sts; rep from * to end (18 sts).

Fill the head/body and keep filling until the last Round.

Round 33: As Round 5.

Round 34: *1 sc (*UK dc*) in next st, dec over next 2 sts; rep from * to end (12 sts).

Round 35: As Round 5.

Round 36: *Dec over next 2 sts; rep from * to end (6 sts).

Tie off with a sl st and close the head/body.

Fins (x2)

Use turquoise blue yarn.

Round 1: 6 sc (*UK dc*) in magic ring (6 sts).

Round 2: 1 sc (UK dc) in each st to end.

Round 3: *1 sc (*UK dc*) in next st, 2 sc (*UK dc*) in next st; rep from * to end (9 sts).

Switch to black yarn.

Round 4: As Round 2.

Round 5: *1 sc (*UK dc*) in next 2 sts, 2 sc (*UK dc*) in next st; rep from * to end (12 sts).

Return to turquoise blue yarn.

Rounds 6 and 7: As Round 2.

Tie off with a sl st, and leave enough yarn to sew the fins to the head/body.

Dorsal fin

Use black yarn.

Work Rounds 1–5 as for fins, working all 5 rounds in black yarn.

Switch to turquoise blue yarn.

Round 6: As Round 2.

Round 7: *1 sc (*UK dc*) in next 3 sts, 2 sc (*UK dc*) in next st; rep from * to end (15 sts).

Round 8: As Round 2.

Round 9: *1 sc (*UK dc*) in next 4 sts, 2 sc (*UK dc*) in next st; rep from * to end (18 sts).

Round 10: As Round 2.

Tie off with a sl st, and leave enough yarn to sew the fin to the head/body.

Star

Use red yarn.

Round 1: 5 sc (*UK dc*) in magic ring (5 sts).

Round 2: *2 ch + 1 tch, turn work, skip tch, 1 sl st in the next ch of 2-ch, 1 sc (*UK dc*) in the next ch of 2-ch, 1 sl st in next st; rep from * four more times, until you have 5 points.

Tie off, and leave enough yarn to sew the star to the head/body.

Tail ring

Use black yarn.

Round 1: 12 ch, sl st in 1st ch made to join the round.

Round 2: 1 sc (*UK dc*) in each st to end (12 sts).

Tie off with a sl st, and leave enough yarn to sew the ring to the head/body.

Tail (x4)

Use green yarn.

Row 1: 16 ch + 1 tch.

Row 2: Turn work, skip tch, 1 sc (*UK dc*) in next 2 ch, 1 sl st in next ch, 2 ch, *1 hdc (*UK htr*) in next ch, 1 sl st in next 2 ch, 2 ch; rep from * to last 4 ch, 1 hdc (*UK htr*) in next ch, 1 sl st in next ch, 1 sc (*UK dc*) in last 2 ch, do not turn.

Continue to work along the other side of the chain as follows: 1 sc (*UK dc*) in next 2 ch, 1 sl st in next ch, 2 ch, *1 hdc (*UK htr*) in next ch, 1 sl st in next ch, 2 ch; rep from * to last 4 ch, 1 hdc (*UK htr*) in next ch, 1 sl st in next ch, 1 sc (*UK dc*) in last 2 ch.

Tie off, and leave enough yarn to sew the tail to the head/body.

Putting all the parts together

Sew the fins to the head/body, at approximately Round 15.

Sew the dorsal fin to the head/body, at approximately Round 17.

Sew the ring to the back of the head/body. Then sew the parts of the tail to the back of the head/body.

Sew the star to the head/body, at approximately Round 9.

Face

Cut 2 eyes out of black, white and red felt and paste these onto the head/body, at approximately Round 10.

Gifly

What you need:

Materials:

4-ply (fine/sport weight) cotton yarn
  light purple, 1 x 50g (1^3/$_4$oz) ball
  yellow, 1 x 50g (1^3/$_4$oz) ball
  red, 1 x 50g (1^3/$_4$oz) ball
  black, small amount
Stuffing (fiberfill)
Black, white and yellow felt

Tools:

2.5mm (UK 13/US B-1) crochet hook
Tapestry (blunt-end) needle

Templates:

Eyes

Black   White

Yellow

Difficulty

Although there are no difficult stitches, the wings can be challenging to make.

Instructions:

Unless stated otherwise, all sections/body parts begin with a magic ring (see page 16 for instructions); the first round should be worked into the ring.

Head/body

Use light purple yarn.

Round 1: 6 sc (*UK dc*) in magic ring (6 sts).

Round 2: 2 sc (*UK dc*) in each st to end (12 sts).

Round 3: *1 sc (*UK dc*) in next st, 2 sc (*UK dc*) in next st; rep from * to end (18 sts).

Round 4: *1 sc (*UK dc*) in next 2 sts, 2 sc (*UK dc*) in next st; rep from * to end (24 sts).

Round 5: *1 sc (*UK dc*) in next 3 sts, 2 sc (UK dc) in next st; rep from * to end (30 sts).

Round 6: *1 sc (*UK dc*) in next 4 sts, 2 sc (*UK dc*) in next st; rep from * to end (36 sts).

Round 7: *1 sc (*UK dc*) in next 5 sts, 2 sc (*UK dc*) in next st; rep from * to end (42 sts).

Rounds 8–14: 1 sc (*UK dc*) in each st to end.

Round 15: *1 sc (*UK dc*) in next 5 sts, dec over next 2 sts; rep from * to end (36 sts).

Round 16: *1 sc (*UK dc*) in next 4 sts, dec over next 2 sts; rep from * to end (30 sts).

Round 17: *1 sc (*UK dc*) in next 3 sts, dec over next 2 sts; rep from * to end (24 sts).

Round 18: *1 sc (*UK dc*) in next 2 sts, dec over next 2 sts; rep from * to end (18 sts).

Fill the head/body and keep filling until the last round.

Rounds 19 and 20: As Rounds 4 and 5 (30 sts).

Rounds 21–25: As Round 14.

Round 26: As Round 17 (24 sts).

Round 27: As Round 14.

Round 28: As Round 18 (18 sts).

Round 29: *1 sc (*UK dc*) in next st, dec over next 2 sts; rep from * to end (12 sts).

Round 30: *Dec over next 2 sts; rep from * to end (6 sts).

Embroider the mouth (see page 79). Tie off with a sl st and close the head/body.

Antennae (x2)

Use yellow yarn.

Row 1: 20 ch + 1 tch.

Row 2: Turn work, skip tch, 1 sc (*UK dc*) in each st to end (20 sts).

Tie off, and leave enough yarn to sew the antennae to the head.

Arms (x2)

Use yellow yarn.

Round 1: 6 sc (*UK dc*) in magic ring (6 sts).

Round 2: 1 sc (*UK dc*) in each st to end.

Round 3: *1 sc (*UK dc*) in next 2 sts, 2 sc (*UK dc*) in next st; rep from * to end (8 sts).

Tie off with a sl st and leave enough yarn to sew the arms to the body.

Feet (x2)

Use yellow yarn.

Round 1: 6 sc (*UK dc*) in magic ring (6 sts).

Round 2: *1 sc (*UK dc*) in next st, 2 sc (*UK dc*) in next st; rep from * to end (9 sts).

Rounds 3–6: 1 sc (*UK dc*) in each st to end.

Round 7: *1 sc (*UK dc*) in next st, dec over next 2 sts; rep from * to end (6 sts).

Fill the feet. Tie off with a sl st, and leave enough yarn to sew the feet to the body.

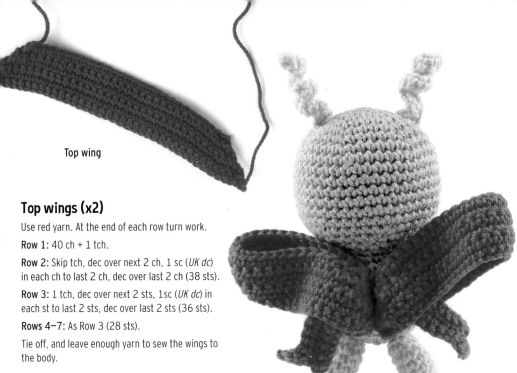

Top wing

Top wings (x2)

Use red yarn. At the end of each row turn work.

Row 1: 40 ch + 1 tch.

Row 2: Skip tch, dec over next 2 ch, 1 sc (*UK dc*) in each ch to last 2 ch, dec over last 2 ch (38 sts).

Row 3: 1 tch, dec over next 2 sts, 1sc (*UK dc*) in each st to last 2 sts, dec over last 2 sts (36 sts).

Rows 4–7: As Row 3 (28 sts).

Tie off, and leave enough yarn to sew the wings to the body.

Bottom wings (x2)

Use red yarn. At the end of each row turn work.

Row 1: 10 ch + 1 tch.

Row 2: Skip tch, 1 sc (*UK dc*) in each st to end (10 sts).

Row 3: 1 tch, 1 sc (*UK dc*) in next 8 sts, work 2 ch + 1 tch and turn, leaving remaining sts unworked.

Row 4: Skip tch, 1 sc (*UK dc*) in each ch and st to end (10 sts).

Tie off, and leave enough yarn to sew this part to the top of the wings.

Bottom wing

Putting all the parts together

Sew the antennae to the head, at approximately Round 4.

Sew the arms to the body, at approximately 3 rounds below the neck.

Sew the feet to the bottom of the body.

Fold first top wing in half. Place a bottom wing between the ends at an angle, sew the bottom wing in place then sew the ends of the top wing together. Repeat for second wing. Sew the wings to the body, at approximately 3 rounds below the neck.

Face

Cut 2 eyes out of black, white and yellow felt and paste these onto the head, at approximately Round 9, with 5 stitches between the eyes.

Embroider a mouth on the head with black yarn, at approximately Round 14. Make sure you do this before you close up the head/body.

Felisky

What you need:

Materials:

4-ply (fine/sport weight) cotton yarn
    light blue, 1 x 50g (1³/₄oz) ball
    white, 1 x 50g (1³/₄oz) ball
Crochet cotton thread, black
Stuffing (fiberfill)
Black and white felt

Tools:

2.5mm (UK 13/US B-1) crochet hook
Tapestry (blunt-end) needle

Templates:

Eyes

Black

White

Nose

Black

Instructions:

Unless stated otherwise, all sections/body parts begin with a magic ring (see page 16 for instructions); the first round should be worked into the ring.

Head

Use light blue yarn.

Round 1: 6 sc (*UK dc*) in magic ring (6 sts).

Round 2: 2 sc (*UK dc*) in each st to end (12 sts).

Round 3: *1 sc (*UK dc*) in next st, 2 sc (*UK dc*) in next st; rep from * to end (18 sts).

Round 4: *1 sc (*UK dc*) in next 2 sts, 2 sc (*UK dc*) in next st; rep from * to end (24 sts).

Round 5: *1 sc (*UK dc*) in next 3 sts, 2 sc (*UK dc*) in next st; rep from * to end (30 sts).

Round 6: *1 sc (*UK dc*) in next 4 sts, 2 sc (*UK dc*) in next st; rep from * to end (36 sts).

Round 7: *1 sc (*UK dc*) in next 5 sts, 2 sc (*UK dc*) in next st; rep from * to end (42 sts).

Rounds 8–13: 1 sc (*UK dc*) in each st to end.

Round 14: 1 sc (*UK dc*) in next 14 sts, *2 sc (*UK dc*) in next st, 1 sc (*UK dc*) in next 2 sts; rep from * five more times, 1 sc (*UK dc*) in each st to end (48 sts).

Rounds 15–17: As Round 13.

Round 18: 1 sc (*UK dc*) in next 14 sts, *dec over next 2 sts, 1 sc (*UK dc*) in next 2 sts; rep from * five more times, 1 sc (*UK dc*) in each st to end (42 sts).

Round 19: *1 sc (*UK dc*) in next 5 sts, dec over next 2 sts; rep from * to end (36 sts).

Round 20: *1 sc (*UK dc*) in next 4 sts, dec over next 2 sts; rep from * to end (30 sts).

Round 21: *1 sc (*UK dc*) in next 3 sts, dec over next 2 sts; rep from * to end (24 sts).

Round 22: *1 sc (*UK dc*) in next 2 sts, dec over next 2 sts; rep from * to end (18 sts).

Round 23: As Round 13.

Fill the head. Embroider the mouth (see page 84). Tie off with a sl st, and leave enough yarn to sew the head to the body.

Body

Use light blue yarn.

Work Rounds 1–4 as for head.

Rounds 5–16: 1 sc (*UK dc*) in each st to end.

Round 17: *1 sc (*UK dc*) in next 2 sts, dec over next 2 sts; rep from * to end (18 sts).

Fill the body and keep filling until the last round.

Round 18: *1 sc (*UK dc*) in next st, dec over next 2 sts; rep from * to end (12 sts).

Round 19: *Dec over next 2 sts; rep from * to end (6 sts).

Tie off with a sl st and close the body.

Forelegs (x2)

Use white yarn.

Round 1: 6 sc (*UK dc*) in magic ring (6 sts).

Round 2: *2 sc (*UK dc*) in each of next 2 sts, 1 sc (*UK dc*) in next st; rep from * to end (10 sts).

Round 3: 1 sc (*UK dc*) in each st to end.

Round 4: [Dec over next 2 sts] twice, 1 sc (*UK dc*) in each st to end (8 sts).

Switch to light blue yarn.

Rounds 5 and 6: As Round 3.

Round 7: *1 sc (*UK dc*) in next 3 sts, 2 sc (*UK dc*) in next st; rep from * to end (10 sts).

Round 8: As Round 3.

Fill the legs. Tie off with a sl st, and leave enough yarn to sew the legs to the body.

Hind legs (x2)

Use white yarn.

Work Rounds 1–6 as for forelegs, switching to light blue yarn after Round 4.

Round 7: *1 sc (*UK dc*) in next st, 2 sc (*UK dc*) in next st; rep from * to end (12 sts).

Rounds 8 and 9: As Round 3.

Fill the legs. Tie off with a sl st, and leave enough yarn to sew the legs to the body.

Tail

Use white yarn.

Work Rounds 1–4 as for head.

Rounds 5–7: 1 sc (*UK dc*) in each st to end.

Round 8: *1 sc (*UK dc*) in next 2 sts, dec over next 2 sts; rep from * to end (18 sts).

Round 9: As Round 4 (24 sts).

Round 10: *1 sc (*UK dc*) in next 3 sts, 2 sc (*UK dc*) in next st; rep from * to end (30 sts).

Round 11: *1 sc (*UK dc*) in next 4 sts, 2 sc (*UK dc*) in next st; rep from * to end (36 sts).

Rounds 12–15: As Round 7.

Round 16: *1 sc (*UK dc*) in next 4 sts, dec over next 2 sts; rep from * to end (30 sts).

Round 17: *1 sc (*UK dc*) in next 3 sts, dec over next 2 sts; rep from * to end (24 sts).

Round 18: As Round 8 (18 sts).

Round 19: As Round 4 (24 sts).

Rounds 20–22: As Round 7.

Round 23: As Round 8 (18 sts).

Round 24: *1 sc (*UK dc*) in next st, dec over next 2 sts; rep from * to end (12 sts).

Fill the tail. Tie off with a sl st and leave enough yarn to sew the tail to the body.

Collar

Use white yarn.

Round 1: 6 sc (*UK dc*) in magic ring (6 sts).

Round 2: 2 sc (*UK dc*) in each st to end (12 sts).

Rounds 3 and 4: 1 sc (*UK dc*) in each st to end.

Round 5: *Dec over next 2 sts; rep from * to end (6 sts).

Repeat Rounds 2–5 a further eight times.

Tie off with a sl st and leave enough yarn to sew the ends together.

Outer ears (x2)

Use light blue yarn.

Round 1: 6 sc (*UK dc*) in magic ring (6 sts).

Round 2: 1 sc (*UK dc*) in each st to end.

Round 3: 2 sc (*UK dc*) in each st to end (12 sts).

Rounds 4 and 5: As Round 2.

Round 6: *1 sc (*UK dc*) in next st, 2 sc (*UK dc*) in next st; rep from * to end (18 sts).

Rounds 7 and 8: As Round 2.

Round 9: *1 sc (*UK dc*) in next 2 sts, 2 sc (*UK dc*) in next st; rep from * to end (24 sts).

Tie off with a sl st, and leave enough yarn to sew the ears to the head.

Inner ears (x2)

Use white yarn.

Row 1: 3 ch + 1 tch.

Row 2: Turn work, skip tch, 1 sl st in next ch, 1 sc (*UK dc*) in next ch, 1 dc (*UK tr*) in last ch.

Tie off with a sl st, and leave enough yarn to sew this part to the outer ears.

Putting all the parts together

Sew the head to the body, at approximately Round 4.

Sew the legs to the body – the forelegs should be at approximately Round 5, and the hind legs at Round 14.

Place the collar around the neck, and sew the ends together.

Sew the tail to the back of the body.

Sew the inner ears onto the outer ears and then sew the ears to the head, at approximately Round 5.

Face

Cut 2 eyes out of black and white felt and paste these onto the head, at approximately Round 10, with 4 stitches between the eyes.

Cut a nose out of black felt and paste it onto the head, at approximately Round 15.

Embroider a mouth on the head with black crochet cotton thread, at approximately Round 17. Make sure you do this before you close up the head.

Washimo

What you need:

Materials:

4-ply (fine/sport weight) cotton yarn
  white, 1 x 50g (1³/₄oz) ball
  dark brown, 1 x 50g (1³/₄oz) ball
  yellow, 1 x 50g (1³/₄oz) ball
  dark green, small amount
Stuffing (fiberfill)
Black, white and green felt

Tools:

2.5mm (UK 13/US B-1) crochet hook
Tapestry (blunt-end) needle

Templates:

Eyes

Black

White

Green

Difficulty

🐾 🐾 🐾 🐾 🐾

For the cowlick and the feathers below the head you need to know hdc (*UK htr*).

Instructions:

Unless stated otherwise, all sections/body parts begin with a magic ring (see page 16 for instructions); the first round should be worked into the ring.

Head

Use white yarn.

Round 1: 6 sc (*UK dc*) in magic ring (6 sts).

Round 2: 2 sc (*UK dc*) in each st to end (12 sts).

Round 3: *1 sc (*UK dc*) in next st, 2 sc (*UK dc*) in next st; rep from * to end (18 sts).

Round 4: *1 sc (*UK dc*) in next 2 sts, 2 sc (*UK dc*) in next st; rep from * to end (24 sts).

Round 5: *1 sc (*UK dc*) in next 3 sts, 2 sc (*UK dc*) in next st; rep from * to end (30 sts).

Round 6: *1 sc (*UK dc*) in next 4 sts, 2 sc (*UK dc*) in next st; rep from * to end (36 sts).

Round 7: *1 sc (*UK dc*) in next 5 sts, 2 sc (*UK dc*) in next st; rep from * to end (42 sts).

Round 8: *1 sc (*UK dc*) in next 6 sts, 2 sc (*UK dc*) in next st; rep from * to end (48 sts).

Rounds 9–16: 1 sc (*UK dc*) in each st to end.

Round 17: *1 sc (*UK dc*) in next 6 sts, dec over next 2 sts; rep from * to end (42 sts).

Round 18: *1 sc (*UK dc*) in next 5 sts, dec over next 2 sts; rep from * to end (36 sts).

Round 19: *1 sc (*UK dc*) in next 4 sts, dec over next 2 sts; rep from * to end (30 sts).

Round 20: *1 sc (*UK dc*) in next 3 sts, dec over next 2 sts; rep from * to end (24 sts).

Round 21: *1 sc (*UK dc*) in next 2 sts, dec over next 2 sts; rep from * to end (18 sts).

Round 22: *1 sl st in next st, work 4 ch + 1 tch, turn work, skip tch, 1 sl st in next ch of 4-ch, 1 sc (*UK dc*) in next ch of 4-ch, 1 hdc (*UK htr*) in next 2 ch of 4-ch, 1 sl st in next st of round; rep from * eight more times, until you have 9 rounded points and all sts have been worked.

Fill the head. Tie off, and leave enough yarn to sew the head to the body.

Body

Use dark brown yarn.

Work Rounds 1–5 as for head.

Rounds 6–10: 1 sc (*UK dc*) in each st to end.

Round 11: *1 sc (*UK dc*) in next 3 sts, dec over next 2 sts; rep from * to end (24 sts).

Round 12: *1 sc (*UK dc*) in next 2 sts, dec over next 2 sts; rep from * to end (18 sts).

Fill the body. Tie off with a sl st.

Wings (x2)

Start with dark brown yarn.

Round 1: 6 sc (*UK dc*) in magic ring (6 sts).

Round 2: 1 sc (*UK dc*) in each st to end.

Round 3: *1 sc (*UK dc*) in next st, 2 sc (*UK dc*) in next st; rep from * to end (9 sts).

Switch to dark green yarn.

Round 4: As Round 2.

Round 5: *1 sc (*UK dc*) in next 2 sts, 2 sc (*UK dc*) in next st; rep from * to end (12 sts).

Switch to white yarn.

Round 6: As Round 2.

Round 7: *1 sc (*UK dc*) in next 3 sts, 2 sc (*UK dc*) in next st; rep from * to end (15 sts).

Switch to dark brown yarn.

Round 8: As Round 2.

Round 9: *1 sc (*UK dc*) in next 3 sts, dec over next 2 sts; rep from * to end (12 sts).

Round 10: *Dec over next 2 sts; rep from * to end (6 sts).

Tie off with a sl st and close the wings. Leave enough yarn to sew the wings to the body.

Feet ››› Part I (x2)

Use yellow yarn.

Round 1: 6 sc (*UK dc*) in magic ring (6 sts).

Round 2: 1 sc (*UK dc*) in each st to end.

Tie off with a sl st.

Feet ››› Part II (x2)

Use yellow yarn.

Work Rounds 1 and 2 as for Part I of feet.

Round 3: Holding Part I of feet next to Part II, work 1 sc (*UK dc*) in each st around Part II then each st around Part I to join (12 sts).

Round 4: *1 sc (*UK dc*) in next 2 sts, dec over next 2 sts; rep from * to end (9 sts).

Round 5: As Round 2.

Round 6: *1 sc (*UK dc*) in next st, dec over next 2 sts; rep from * to end (6 sts).

Tie off with a sl st and close the feet. Leave enough yarn to sew the feet to the body.

Tail ››› Part I (x2)

Use dark green yarn.

Round 1: 6 sc (*UK dc*) in magic ring (6 sts).

Round 2: *1 sc (*UK dc*) in next 2 sts, 2 sc (*UK dc*) in next st; rep from * to end (8 sts).

Round 3: 1 sc (*UK dc*) in each st to end.

Tie off with a sl st.

Tail ››› Part II (x2)

Use dark green yarn.

Work Rounds 1–3 as for Part I of tail.

Tie off with a sl st.

Tail ››› Part III (x2)

Start with dark green yarn,

Work Rounds 1–3 as for Parts I and II of tail.

Round 4: Hold the three parts together and join tail as follows: 1 sc (*UK dc*) in first 4 sts of Part I, 1 sc (*UK dc*) in each st around of Part II, 1 sc (*UK dc*) in last 4 sts of Part I, 1 sc (*UK dc*) in each st around of Part III (24 sts).

Round 5: *1 sc (*UK dc*) in next 6 sts, dec over next 2 sts; rep from * to end (21 sts).

Switch to white yarn.

Round 6: 1 sc (*UK dc*) in each st to end.

Round 7: *1 sc (*UK dc*) in next 5 sts, dec over next 2 sts; rep from * to end (18 sts).

Switch to dark brown yarn.

Round 8: As Round 6.

Round 9: *1 sc (*UK dc*) in next st, dec over next 2 sts; rep from * to end (12 sts).

Round 10: As Round 6.

Tie off with a sl st, and leave enough yarn to sew the tail to the body.

Beak

Use yellow yarn.

Round 1: 6 sc (*UK dc*) in magic ring (6 sts).

Round 2: 1 sc (*UK dc*) in each st to end.

Round 3: 2 sc (*UK dc*) in each st to end (12 sts).

Round 4: As Round 2.

Round 5: *1 sc (*UK dc*) in next st, 2 sc (*UK dc*) in next st; rep from * to end (18 sts).

Round 6: As Round 2.

Round 7: [Dec over next 2 sts] four times, leave remaining sts unworked (14 sts).

Fill the beak. Tie off with a sl st, and leave enough yarn to sew the beak to the head.

Cowlick

Use white yarn.

Round 1: 6 sc (*UK dc*) in magic ring, turn (6 sts).

Round 2: 1 tch, then:

- **Step 1:** 1 sl st in next st, work 3 ch + 1 tch, turn work, skip tch, 1 sl st in next ch of 3-ch, 1 sc (*UK dc*) in next ch of 3-ch, 1 hdc (*UK htr*) in last ch of 3-ch, 1 sl st in next st

- **Step 2:** 1 sl st in next st, work 4 ch + 1 tch, turn work, skip tch, 1 sl st in next ch of 4-ch, 1 sc (*UK dc*) in next ch of 4-ch, 1 hdc (*UK htr*) in next ch of 4-ch, 1 dc (*UK tr*) in last ch of 4-ch, 1 sl st in next st

- **Step 3:** Repeat Step 1 once more.

Tie off and leave enough yarn to sew the cowlick to the head.

Putting all the parts together

Sew the head to the body.

Sew the wings to the body, just below the head.

Sew the feet to the bottom of the body.

Sew the tail to the body, at approximately Round 6 (counted from above).

Sew the beak to the head, at approximately Round 12.

Sew the cowlick to the top of the head.

Face

Cut 2 eyes out of black, white and green felt and paste these onto the head, at approximately Round 9, with 9 stitches between the eyes.

Corell

What you need:

Materials:

4-ply (fine/sport weight) cotton yarn
  blue, 1 x 50g (1³/₄oz) ball
  pink, 1 x 50g (1³/₄oz) ball
  off white, 1 x 50g (1³/₄oz) ball
Stuffing (fiberfill)
Blue, black and white felt

Tools:

2.5mm (UK 13/US B-1) crochet hook
Tapestry (blunt-end) needle

Templates:

Eyes

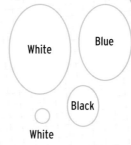

White

Blue

Black

White

Difficulty

To get the shape of the head, it is important to follow the instructions for increase and decrease in specific stitches.

Instructions:

Unless stated otherwise, all sections/body parts begin with a magic ring (see page 16 for instructions); the first round should be worked into the ring.

Head

Use blue yarn.

Round 1: 6 sc (*UK dc*) in magic ring (6 sts).

Round 2: 2 sc (*UK dc*) in each st to end (12 sts).

Round 3: *1 sc (*UK dc*) in next st, 2 sc (*UK dc*) in next st; rep from * to end (18 sts).

Round 4: *1 sc (*UK dc*) in next 2 sts, 2 sc (*UK dc*) in next st; rep from * to end (24 sts).

Round 5: *1 sc (*UK dc*) in next 3 sts, 2 sc (*UK dc*) in next st; rep from * to end (30 sts).

Round 6: *1 sc (*UK dc*) in next 4 sts, 2 sc (*UK dc*) in next st; rep from * to end (36 sts).

Round 7: *1 sc (*UK dc*) in next 5 sts, 2 sc (*UK dc*) in next st; rep from * to end (42 sts).

Round 8: *1 sc (*UK dc*) in next 6 sts, 2 sc (*UK dc*) in next st; rep from * to end (48 sts).

Rounds 9–14: 1 sc (*UK dc*) in each st to end.

Round 15: 1 sc (*UK dc*) in next 17 sts, *2 sc (*UK dc*) in next st, 1 sc (*UK dc*) in next 2 sts; rep from * five more times, 1 sc (*UK dc*) in each st to end (54 sts).

Rounds 16–18: As Round 14.

Round 19: 1 sc (*UK dc*) in next 17 sts, *dec over next 2 sts, 1 sc (*UK dc*) in next 2 sts; rep from * five more times, 1 sc (*UK dc*) in each st to end (48 sts).

Round 20: *1 sc (*UK dc*) in next 6 sts, dec over next 2 sts; rep from * to end (42 sts).

Round 21: *1 sc (*UK dc*) in next 5 sts, dec over next 2 sts; rep from * to end (36 sts).

Round 22: *1 sc (*UK dc*) in next 4 sts, dec over next 2 sts; rep from * to end (30 sts).

Round 23: *1 sc (*UK dc*) in next 3 sts, dec over next 2 sts; rep from * to end (24 sts).

Round 24: *1 sc (*UK dc*) in next 2 sts, dec over next 2 sts; rep from * to end (18 sts).

Round 25: *1 sc (*UK dc*) in next st, dec over next 2 sts; rep from * to end (12 sts).

Round 26: *Dec over next 2 sts; rep from * to end (6 sts).

Tie off with a sl st and close the head.

Shell

Use pink yarn.

Work Rounds 1–7 as for head.

Round 8: 1 sc (*UK dc*) in each st to end.

Round 9: *1 sc (*UK dc*) in next 6 sts, 2 sc (*UK dc*) in next st; rep from * to end (48 sts).

Round 10: 1 sc (*UK dc*) in each st to end, alternating between pink and off-white yarn every 4 sts.

Continue with off-white yarn only.

Rounds 11 and 12: As Round 8.

Round 13: *1 sc (*UK dc*) in next 6 sts, dec over next 2 sts; rep from * to end (42 sts).

Round 14: *1 sc (*UK dc*) in next 5 sts, dec over next 2 sts; rep from * to end (36 sts).

Round 15: *1 sc (*UK dc*) in next 4 sts, dec over next 2 sts; rep from * to end (30 sts).

Round 16: *1 sc (*UK dc*) in next 3 sts, dec over next 2 sts; rep from * to end (24 sts).

Round 17: *1 sc (*UK dc*) in next 2 sts, dec over next 2 sts; rep from * to end (18 sts).

Fill the shell and keep filling until the last round.

Round 18: *1 sc (*UK dc*) in next st, dec over next 2 sts; rep from * to end (12 sts).

Round 19: *Dec over next 2 sts; rep from * to end (6 sts).

Tie off with a sl st and close the shell.

Shell edging

Use off–white yarn.

Row 1: 70 ch + 1 tch.

Row 2: Turn work, skip tch, 1 sc (*UK dc*) in each ch to end (70 sts).

Tie off, and leave enough yarn to sew the edge to the shell.

Coral polyp (x3)

Use pink yarn.

Round 1: 6 sc (*UK dc*) in magic ring (6 sts).

Round 2: *1 sc (*UK dc*) in next st, 2 sc (*UK dc*) in next st; rep from * to end (9 sts).

Rounds 3–7: 1 sc (*UK dc*) in each st to end.

Round 8: *1 sc (*UK dc*) in next 2 sts, 2 sc (*UK dc*) in next st; rep from * to end (12 sts).

Rounds 9 and 10: As Round 7.

Tie off with a sl st, and leave enough yarn to sew the coral to the shell.

Coral tentacles (x6)

Use pink yarn.

Round 1: 6 sc (*UK dc*) in magic ring (6 sts).

Rounds 2–4: 1 sc (*UK dc*) in each st to end.

Tie off with a sl st, and leave enough yarn to sew the sides to the middle parts.

Front feet (x2)

Use blue yarn.

Round 1: 6 sc (*UK dc*) in magic ring. (6 sts).

Round 2: 1 sc (*UK dc*) in each st to end.

Round 3: *1 sc (*UK dc*) in next st, 2 sc (*UK dc*) in next st; rep from * to end (9 sts).

Round 4: As Round 2.

Round 5: *1 sc (*UK dc*) in next 2 sts, 2 sc (*UK dc*) in next st; rep from * to end (12 sts).

Round 6: *1 sc (*UK dc*) in next 3 sts, 2 sc (*UK dc*) in next st; rep from * to end (15 sts).

Rounds 7 and 8: As Round 2.

Round 9: *1 sc (*UK dc*) in next 3 sts, dec over next 2 sts; rep from * to end (12 sts).

Round 10: As Round 2.

Round 11: *1 sc (*UK dc*) in next st, dec over next 2 sts; rep from * to end (8 sts).

Tie off with a sl st, and leave enough yarn to sew the fins to the shell.

Back feet (x2)

Use blue yarn.

Work Rounds 1–7 as for front feet.

Round 8: *1 sc (*UK dc*) in next 3 sts, dec over next 2 sts; rep from * to end (12 sts).

Round 9: *1 sc (*UK dc*) in next st, dec over next 2 sts; rep from * to end (8 sts).

Tie off with a sl st and leave enough yarn to sew the fins to the shell.

Putting all the parts together

Sew the head to the shell.

Sew the feet to the shell, at approximately Round 13.

Sew the edge around the shell, at approximately Round 12.

Sew 2 coral tentacles to opposite sides of each polyp, at approximately Round 6 and 7.

Finally, sew the coral to the shell.

Face

Cut 2 eyes out of white, blue and black felt and paste these onto the head, at approximately Round 8, with 11 stitches between the eyes.

Lunax

What you need:

Materials:

4-ply (fine/sport weight) cotton yarn
   dark grey 1 x 50g ($1^3/_4$oz) ball
   black, 1 x 50g ($1^3/_4$oz) ball
   medium grey, small amount
Crochet cotton thread, black
Stuffing (fiberfill)
Black, white and grey felt

Tools:

2.5mm (UK 13/US B-1) crochet hook
Tapestry (blunt-end) needle

Templates:

Eyes

Black

White

Grey

Teeth

▽ White

Instructions:

Unless stated otherwise, all sections/body parts begin with a magic ring (see page 16 for instructions); the first round should be worked into the ring.

Head/body

Use dark grey yarn.

Round 1: 6 sc (*UK dc*) in magic ring (6 sts).

Round 2: 2 sc (*UK dc*) in each st to end (12 sts).

Round 3: *1 sc (*UK dc*) in next st, 2 sc (*UK dc*) in next st; rep from * to end (18 sts).

Round 4: *1 sc (*UK dc*) in next 2 sts, 2 sc (*UK dc*) in next st; rep from * to end (24 sts).

Round 5: *1 sc (*UK dc*) in next 3 sts, 2 sc (*UK dc*) in next st; rep from * to end (30 sts).

Round 6: *1 sc (*UK dc*) in next 4 sts, 2 sc (*UK dc*) in next st; rep from * to end (36 sts).

Round 7: *1 sc (*UK dc*) in next 5 sts, 2 sc (*UK dc*) in next st; rep from * to end (42 sts).

Round 8: *1 sc (*UK dc*) in next 6 sts, 2 sc (*UK dc*) in next st; rep from * to end (48 sts).

Rounds 9–16: 1 sc (*UK dc*) in each st to end.

Round 17: *1 sc (*UK dc*) in next 6 sts, dec over next 2 sts; rep from * to end (42 sts).

Round 18: *1 sc (*UK dc*) in next 5 sts, dec over next 2 sts; rep from * to end (36 sts).

Round 19: *1 sc (*UK dc*) in next 4 sts, dec over next 2 sts; rep from * to end (30 sts).

Round 20: *1 sc (*UK dc*) in next 3 sts, dec over next 2 sts; rep from * to end (24 sts).

Round 21: As Round 5 (30 sts).

Rounds 22–26: As Round 16.

Round 27: As Round 20 (24 sts).

Round 28: *1 sc (*UK dc*) in next 2 sts, dec over next 2 sts; rep from * to end (18 sts).

Fill the head/body and keep filling until the last round.

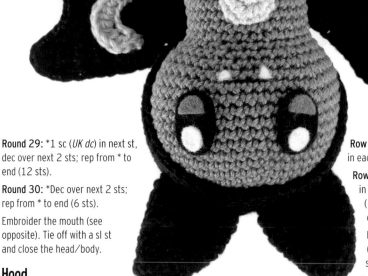

Round 29: *1 sc (*UK dc*) in next st, dec over next 2 sts; rep from * to end (12 sts).

Round 30: *Dec over next 2 sts; rep from * to end (6 sts).

Embroider the mouth (see opposite). Tie off with a sl st and close the head/body.

Hood

Use black yarn.

Work Rounds 1–15 as for head/body.

Tie off with a sl st.

Ears (x2)

Use black yarn.

Round 1: 6 sc (*UK dc*) in magic ring (6 sts).

Round 2: *1 sc (*UK dc*) in next st, 2 sc (*UK dc*) in next st; rep from * to end (9 sts).

Round 3: 1 sc (*UK dc*) in each st to end.

Round 4: *1 sc (*UK dc*) in next 2 sts, 2 sc (*UK dc*) in next st; rep from * to end (12 sts).

Round 5: As Round 3.

Round 6: *1 sc (*UK dc*) in next 3 sts, 2 sc (*UK dc*) in next st; rep from * to end (15 sts).

Round 7: As Round 3.

Round 8: *1 sc (*UK dc*) in next 4 sts, 2 sc (*UK dc*) in next st; rep from * to end (18 sts).

Rounds 9–11: As Round 3.

Tie off with a sl st, and leave enough yarn to sew the ears to the head.

Wings (x4)

Use black yarn. At the end of each row turn work.

Row 1: 1 ch + 1 tch.

Row 2: Skip tch, 2 sc (*UK dc*) in next ch (2 sts).

Row 3: 1 tch, 1 sc (*UK dc*) in next st, 2 sc (*UK dc*) in last st (3 sts).

Row 4: 1 tch, 1 sc (*UK dc*) in each st to end.

Row 5: 1 tch, 1 sc (*UK dc*) in each st to last st, 2 sc (*UK dc*) in last st, work 3 ch + 1 tch.

Row 6: Skip tch, 1 sc (*UK dc*) in each ch and st to end (7 sts).

Rows 7 and 8: As Row 4.

Row 9: 1 tch, 1 sc (*UK dc*) in each st to end, work 3 ch + 1 tch.

Row 10: As Row 6 (10 sts).

Row 11: 1 tch, dec over next 2 sts, 1 sc (*UK dc*) in each st to end (9 sts).

Row 12: 1 tch, 1 sc (*UK dc*) in each st to last 2 sts, dec over last 2 sts (8 sts).

Repeat Rows 11 and 12 twice more, then repeat Row 11 only once more (3 sts).

Rows 18 and 19: As Row 4.

Tie off. Hold 2 wing pieces together and work a row of sc (*UK dc*) around entire edge to join. Repeat for other wing. Leave enough yarn to sew the wings to the body.

Crescent-moon shapes (x2)

Use medium grey yarn.

Row 1: 6 ch + 1 tch.

Row 2: Turn work, skip tch, 1 sl st in next ch, 2 sc (*UK dc*) in next ch, 2 hdc (*UK htr*) in each of next 2 ch, 2 sc (*UK dc*) in next ch, 1 sl st in last ch (10 sts).

Tie off, and leave enough yarn to sew the moons to the wings.

Feet (x2)

Use dark grey yarn.

Work Rounds 1–5 as for ears.

Fill the feet. Tie off with a sl st, and leave enough yarn to sew the feet to the body.

Belly

Use medium grey yarn.

Work Rounds 1 and 2 as for head/body.

Tie off with a sl st, and leave enough yarn to sew the belly to the body.

Putting all the parts together

Place the hood on the head, then sew the ears to the hood, going through to the head on some stitches to secure the hood to the head.

Sew the feet to the bottom of the body.

Sew the belly to the body, approximately 3 rounds below the neck.

Sew the moons onto the wings then sew the wings to the body, approximately 2 rounds below the neck.

Face

Cut 2 eyes out of black, white and grey felt and paste these onto the head, at approximately Round 9.

Embroider a mouth on the head with black crochet cotton thread, at approximately Round 15. Make sure you do this before you close up the head/body.

Cut 2 teeth out of white felt and paste these onto the head, just below the mouth.

Stegoroc

What you need:

Materials:

4-ply (fine/sport weight) cotton yarn
  beige, 1 x 50g (1³/₄oz) ball
  dark brown, 1 x 50g (1³/₄oz) ball
  light grey, small amount
Stuffing (fiberfill)
Black and white felt

Tools:

2.5mm (UK 13/US B-1) crochet hook
Tapestry (blunt-end) needle

Templates:

Eyes

Black   White

Nostrils

⬭ Black

Difficulty

🦕 🦕 🦕 🦕 🦕

No difficult stitches. Only
need sc (*UK dc*), sl st and ch.

Instructions:

Unless stated otherwise, all sections/body parts begin with a magic ring (see page 16 for instructions); the first round should be worked into the ring.

Head

Use beige yarn.

Round 1: 6 sc (*UK dc*) in magic ring (6 sts).

Round 2: 2 sc (*UK dc*) in each st to end (12 sts).

Round 3: *1 sc (*UK dc*) in next st, 2 sc (*UK dc*) in next st; rep from * to end (18 sts).

Round 4: *1 sc (*UK dc*) in next 2 sts, 2 sc (*UK dc*) in next st; rep from * to end (24 sts).

Round 5: 1 sc (*UK dc*) in each st to end.

Round 6: *1 sc (*UK dc*) in next 3 sts, 2 sc (UK dc) in next st; rep from * to end (30 sts).

Round 7: As Round 5.

Round 8: *1 sc (*UK dc*) in next 4 sts, 2 sc (*UK dc*) in next st; rep from * to end (36 sts).

Round 9: As Round 5.

Round 10: *1 sc (*UK dc*) in next 5 sts, 2 sc (*UK dc*) in next st; rep from * to end (42 sts).

Round 11: *1 sc (*UK dc*) in next 6 sts, 2 sc (*UK dc*) in next st; rep from * to end (48 sts).

Rounds 12–15: As Round 5.

Round 16: *1 sc (*UK dc*) in next 6 sts, dec over next 2 sts; rep from * to end (42 sts).

Round 17: As Round 5.

Round 18: *1 sc (*UK dc*) in next 5 sts, dec over next 2 sts; rep from * to end (36 sts).

Round 19: As Round 5.

Round 20: *1 sc (*UK dc*) in next 4 sts, dec over next 2 sts; rep from * to end (30 sts).

Round 21: *1 sc (*UK dc*) in next 3 sts, dec over next 2 sts; rep from * to end (24 sts).

Round 22: *1 sc (*UK dc*) in next 2 sts, dec over next 2 sts; rep from * to end (18 sts).

Fill the head and keep filling until the last round.

Round 23: *1 sc (*UK dc*) in next st, dec over next 2 sts; rep from * to end (12 sts).

Round 24: *Dec over next 2 sts; rep from * to end (6 sts).

Tie off with a sl st and close the head.

Body

Use beige yarn.

Work Rounds 1–4 as for head.

Round 5: *1 sc (*UK dc*) in next 3 sts, 2 sc (*UK dc*) in next st; rep from * to end (30 sts).

Rounds 6–15: 1 sc (*UK dc*) in each st to end.

Round 16: *1 sc (*UK dc*) in next 3 sts, dec over next 2 sts; rep from * to end (24 sts).

Round 17: *1 sc (*UK dc*) in next 2 sts, dec over next 2 sts; rep from * to end (18 sts).

Fill the body and keep filling until the last round.

Round 18: *1 sc (*UK dc*) in next st, dec over next 2 sts; rep from * to end (12 sts).

Round 19: *Dec over next 2 sts; rep from * to end (6 sts).

Tie off with a sl st and close the body.

Tail

Use beige yarn.

Round 1: 6 sc (*UK dc*) in magic ring (6 sts).

Round 2: 1 sc (*UK dc*) in each st to end.

Round 3: *1 sc (*UK dc*) in next st, 2 sc (*UK dc*) in next st; rep from * to end (9 sts).

Rounds 4 and 5: As Round 2.

Round 6: *1 sc (*UK dc*) in next 2 sts, 2 sc (*UK dc*) in next st; rep from * to end (12 sts).

Rounds 7 and 8: As Round 2.

Round 9: *1 sc (*UK dc*) in next 3 sts, 2 sc (*UK dc*) in next st; rep from * to end (15 sts).

Rounds 10 and 11: As Round 2.

Round 12: *1 sc (*UK dc*) in next 4 sts, 2 sc (*UK dc*) in next st; rep from * to end (18 sts).

Fill the tail. Tie off with a sl st and leave enough yarn to sew the tail to the body.

Legs (x4)

Use beige yarn.

Work Rounds 1 and 2 as for head.

Round 3: Working in back loops only, 1 sc (*UK dc*) in each st to end.

Rounds 4 and 5: 1 sc (*UK dc*) in each st to end.

Round 6: *1 sc (*UK dc*) in next 4 sts, dec over next 2 sts; rep from * to end (10 sts).

Round 7: As Round 5.

Fill the legs. Tie off with a sl st, and leave enough yarn to sew the legs to the body.

Stone plates (x5)

Use light grey yarn.

Work Rounds 1 and 2 as for tail.

Round 3: 2 sc (*UK dc*) in each st to end (12 sts).

Round 4: As Round 2.

Round 5: *1 sc (*UK dc*) in next st, dec over next 2 sts; rep from * to end (8 sts).

Round 6: As Round 2.

Tie off with a sl st and leave enough yarn to sew the plates to the stripe.

Stripe

Use dark brown yarn. At the end of each row turn work.

Row 1: 2 ch + 1 tch.

Row 2: Skip tch, 2 sc (*UK dc*) in each ch to end (4 sts).

Rows 3 and 4: 1 tch, 1 sc (*UK dc*) in each st to end.

Row 5: 1 tch, 2 sc (*UK dc*) in next st, 1 sc (*UK dc*) in each st to last st, 2 sc (*UK dc*) in last st (6 sts).

Rows 6 and 7: As Rows 3 and 4.

Rows 8–16: Repeat Rows 5–7 three more times (12 sts).

Rows 17–29: As Rows 3 and 4.

Row 30: 1 tch, dec over next 2 sts, 1 sc (*UK dc*) in each st to last 2 sts, dec over last 2 sts (10 sts).

Rows 31 and 32: As Rows 3 and 4.

Rows 33–35: Repeat Rows 30–32 once more (8 sts).

Rows 36–39: Repeat Rows 30 and 31 twice more (4 sts).

Row 40: 1 tch, [dec over next 2 sts] twice (2 sts).

Row 41: As Rows 3 and 4.

Row 42: 1 tch, dec over next 2 sts (1 st).

Tie off, and leave enough yarn to sew the stripe to the tail, body and head.

Putting all the parts together

Sew the head to the body.

Sew the tail to the back of the body.

Sew the legs to the body – the forelegs at approximately Round 5, and the hind legs at Round 12.

Sew the stripe to the top of the tail, body and head.

Sew 2 stone plates to the stripe on the body and 3 stone plates to the stripe on the head.

Face

Cut 2 eyes out of black and white felt, and paste these onto the head, at approximately Round 8, with 11 stitches between the eyes.

Cut 2 nostrils out of black felt and paste these onto the head, at approximately Round 3.

Duplicorn

What you need:

Materials:

4-ply (fine/sport weight) cotton yarn
  light brown 1 x 50g (1³/₄oz) ball
  dark brown, 1 x 50g (1³/₄oz) ball
  green, small amount
  orange, small amount
Stuffing (fiberfill)
Black and white felt

Tools:

2.5mm (UK 13/US B-1) crochet hook
Tapestry (blunt-end) needle

Templates:

Eyes

Black   White

Difficulty

Although there are no difficult stitches, the leaves can be challenging to make.

Instructions:

Unless stated otherwise, all sections/body parts begin with a magic ring (see page 16 for instructions); the first round should be worked into the ring.

Heads/bodies (x2)

Use light brown yarn.

Round 1: 6 sc (*UK dc*) in magic ring (6 sts).

Round 2: 1 sc (*UK dc*) in each st to end.

Round 3: 2 sc (*UK dc*) in each st to end (12 sts).

Round 4: *1 sc (*UK dc*) in next st, 2 sc (*UK dc*) in next st; rep from * to end (18 sts).

Round 5: *1 sc (*UK dc*) in next 2 sts, 2 sc (*UK dc*) in next st; rep from * to end (24 sts).

Round 6: *1 sc (*UK dc*) in next 3 sts, 2 sc (*UK dc*) in next st; rep from * to end (30 sts).

Round 7: *1 sc (*UK dc*) in next 4 sts, 2 sc (*UK dc*) in next st; rep from * to end (36 sts).

Round 8: *1 sc (*UK dc*) in next 5 sts, 2 sc (*UK dc*) in next st; rep from * to end (42 sts).

Rounds 9–16: As Round 2.

Round 17: *1 sc (*UK dc*) in next 5 sts, dec over next 2 sts; rep from * to end (36 sts).

Round 18: *1 sc (*UK dc*) in next 4 sts, dec over next 2 sts; rep from * to end (30 sts).

Round 19: *1 sc (*UK dc*) in next 3 sts, dec over next 2 sts; rep from * to end (24 sts).

Round 20: *1 sc (*UK dc*) in next 2 sts, dec over next 2 sts; rep from * to end (18 sts).

Fill the heads/bodies and keep filling until the last round.

Round 21: *1 sc (*UK dc*) in next st, dec over next 2 sts; rep from * to end (12 sts).

Round 22: *Dec over next 2 sts; rep from * to end (6 sts).

Tie off with a sl st and close the heads/bodies.

Feet (x4)

Use light brown yarn.

Round 1: 6 sc (*UK dc*) in magic ring (6 sts).

Round 2: *1 sc (*UK dc*) in next st, 2 sc (*UK dc*) in next st; rep from * to end (9 sts).

Rounds 3–5: 1 sc (*UK dc*) in each st to end.

Round 6: *1 sc (*UK dc*) in next st, dec over next 2 sts; rep from * to end (6 sts).

Tie off with a sl st and close the feet. Leave enough yarn to sew the feet to the heads/bodies.

Caps (x2)

Use dark brown yarn.

Round 1: 6 sc (*UK dc*) in magic ring (6 sts).

Rounds 2–7: Work as Rounds 3–8 of heads/bodies (42 sts).

Rounds 8–11: 1 sc (*UK dc*) in each st to end.

Tie off with a sl st.

Stem ››› Part I

Use dark brown yarn.

Leave enough yarn at the beginning to sew the stem to the caps.

Round 1: 6 ch, 1 sl st in 1st chain made to join the round.

Round 2: 1 sc (*UK dc*) in each ch to end (6 sts).

Rounds 3–9: 1 sc (*UK dc*) in each st to end.

Tie off with a sl st.

Stem ››› Part II

Use dark brown yarn.

Leave enough yarn at the beginning to sew the stem to the caps.

Work Rounds 1–9 as for Part I of stem.

Round 10: Holding Part I of stem next to Part II, work 1 sc (*UK dc*) in each st around Part II, then each st around Part I to join (12 sts).

Rounds 11 and 12: 1 sc (*UK dc*) in each st to end.

Round 13: *Dec over next 2 sts; rep from * to end (6 sts).

Tie off with a sl st and close the stem.

Leaves (x2)

Use green and orange yarn, making 1 of each colour.

Row 1: 15 ch + 1 tch.

Row 2: Turn work, skip tch, *1 sc (*UK dc*) in next 3 ch, work 2 ch + 1 tch, turn work, skip tch, 1 hdc (*UK htr*) in each ch of 2-ch; rep from * to last 3 ch, 1 sc (*UK dc*) in last 3 ch, do not turn.

Work 2 ch, then continue to work along the other side of the chain as follows: *1 sc (*UK dc*) in next 3 ch, work 2 ch + 1 tch, turn work, skip tch, 1 hdc (*UK htr*) in each ch of 2-ch; rep from * to last 3 ch, 1 sc (*UK dc*) in last 3 ch.

Tie off with a sl st, and leave enough yarn to sew the leaves to the stem.

Putting all the parts together

Sew the feet to the bottom of the heads/bodies.

Sew the stem to the top of the caps. Sew the leaves to the stem.

Sew the caps at an askew angle onto the heads/bodies.

Face

Cut 2 eyes out of black and white felt for each acorn and paste these onto the heads/bodies, at approximately Round 11, with 4 stitches between the eyes.

105

Longnoh

Materials:

4-ply (fine/sport weight) cotton yarn
  red, 1 x 50g (1³/₄oz) ball
  yellow, 1 x 50g (1³/₄oz)ball
3-ply (light fingering) acrylic yarn
  orange, small amount
  yellow, small amount
Stuffing (fiberfill)
Black and white felt

Tools:

2.5mm (UK 13/US B-1) crochet hook
Tapestry (blunt-end) needle
Fine-toothed brush, like a slicker brush

Templates:

Eyes

White

Black

White

Difficulty

For the wings it is important to follow the rows carefully.

Instructions:

Unless stated otherwise, all sections/body parts begin with a magic ring (see page 16 for instructions); the first round should be worked into the ring.

Head

Use red yarn.

Round 1: 6 sc (*UK dc*) in magic ring (6 sts).

Round 2: 2 sc (*UK dc*) in each st to end (12 sts).

Round 3: *1 sc (*UK dc*) in next st, 2 sc (*UK dc*) in next st; rep from * to end (18 sts).

Rounds 4 and 5: 1 sc (*UK dc*) in each st to end.

Round 6: *1 sc (*UK dc*) in next 2 sts, 2 sc (*UK dc*) in next st; rep from * to end (24 sts).

Round 7: As Round 5.

Round 8: *1 sc (*UK dc*) in next 3 sts, 2 sc (*UK dc*) in next st; rep from * to end (30 sts).

Round 9: As Round 5.

Round 10: *1 sc (*UK dc*) in next 4 sts, 2 sc (*UK dc*) in next st; rep from * to end (36 sts).

Round 11: *1 sc (*UK dc*) in next 5 sts, 2 sc (*UK dc*) in next st; rep from * to end (42 sts).

Round 12: *1 sc (*UK dc*) in next 6 sts, 2 sc (*UK dc*) in next st; rep from * to end (48 sts).

Rounds 13–15: As Round 5.

Round 16: *1 sc (*UK dc*) in next 6 sts, dec over next 2 sts; rep from * to end (42 sts).

Round 17: As Round 5.

Round 18: *1 sc (*UK dc*) in next 5 sts, dec over next 2 sts; rep from * to end (36 sts).

Round 19: As Round 5.

Round 20: *1 sc (*UK dc*) in next 4 sts, dec over next 2 sts; rep from * to end (30 sts).

Round 21: *1 sc (*UK dc*) in next 3 sts, dec over next 2 sts; rep from * to end (24 sts).

Round 22: *1 sc (*UK dc*) in next 2 sts, dec over next 2 sts; rep from * to end (18 sts).

Fill the head and keep filling until the last round.

Round 23: *1 sc (*UK dc*) in next st, dec over next 2 sts; rep from * to end (12 sts).

Round 24: *Dec over next 2 sts; rep from * to end (6 sts).

Tie off with a sl st and close the head.

Body

Use red yarn.

Work Rounds 1–3 as for head.

Round 4: *1 sc (*UK dc*) in next 2 sts, 2 sc (*UK dc*) in next st; rep from * to end (24 sts).

Round 5: *1 sc (*UK dc*) in next 3 sts, 2 sc (*UK dc*) in next st; rep from * to end (30 sts).

Rounds 6–9: 1 sc (*UK dc*) in each st to end.

Round 10: *1 sc (*UK dc*) in next 3 sts, dec over next 2 sts; rep from * to end (24 sts).

Rounds 11 and 12: As Round 9.

Round 13: *1 sc (*UK dc*) in next 2 sts, dec over next 2 sts; rep from * to end (18 sts).

Rounds 14–16: As Round 9.

Fill the body. Tie off with a sl st, and leave enough yarn to sew the body to the head.

Belly

Use yellow yarn. At the end of each row turn work.

Row 1: 2 ch + 1 tch.

Row 2: Skip tch, 1 sc (*UK dc*) in each ch to end (2 sts).

Row 3: 1 tch, 1 sc (*UK dc*) in each st to end.

Row 4: 1 tch, 2 sc (*UK dc*) in each st to end (4 sts).

Row 5: 1 tch, 2 sc (*UK dc*) in next st, 1 sc (*UK dc*) in each st to last st, 2 sc (*UK dc*) in last st (6 sts).

Rows 6–9: As Row 3.

Row 10: 1 tch, dec over next 2 sts, 1 sc (*UK dc*) in each st to last 2 sts, dec over last 2 sts (4 sts).

Row 11: As Row 3.

Row 12: 1 tch, [dec over next 2 sts] twice (2 sts).

Tie off, and leave enough yarn to sew the belly to the body.

Arms (x2)

Use red yarn.

Round 1: 6 sc (*UK dc*) in magic ring (6 sts).

Round 2: *1 sc (*UK dc*) in next st, 2 sc (*UK dc*) in next st; rep from * to end (9 sts).

Rounds 3–7: 1 sc (*UK dc*) in each st to end.

Fill the arms. Tie off with a sl st, and leave enough yarn to sew the arms to the body.

Legs (x2)

Use red yarn.

Work Rounds 1 and 2 as for head.

Round 3: *1 sc (*UK dc*) in next 3 sts, 2 sc (*UK dc*) in next st; rep from * to end (15 sts).

Rounds 4–6: 1 sc (*UK dc*) in each st to end.

Round 7: *1 sc (*UK dc*) in next 3 sts, dec over next 2 sts; rep from * to end (12 sts).

Round 8: As Round 6.

Round 9: *1 sc (*UK dc*) in next 2 sts, dec over next 2 sts; rep from * to end (9 sts).

Tie off with a sl st, and leave enough yarn to sew the legs to the body.

Feet (x2)

Use red yarn.

Round 1: 6 sc (*UK dc*) in magic ring (6 sts).

Round 2: *1 sc (*UK dc*) in next 2 sts, 2 sc (*UK dc*) in next st; rep from * to end (8 sts).

Rounds 3–6: 1 sc (*UK dc*) in each st to end.

Round 7: *1 sc (*UK dc*) in next 2 sts, dec over next 2 sts; rep from * to end (6 sts).

Tie off with a sl st and close the feet. Leave enough yarn to sew the feet to the legs.

Tail

Use red yarn.

Work Rounds 1–5 as for large horns.

Round 6: As Round 2.

Round 7: *1 sc (*UK dc*) in next 2 sts, 2 sc (*UK dc*) in next st; rep from * to end (12 sts).

Rounds 8–10: As Round 2.

Round 11: *1 sc (*UK dc*) in next 3 sts, 2 sc (*UK dc*) in next st; rep from * to end (15 sts).

Rounds 12–14: As Round 2.

Fill the tail. Tie off with a sl st, and leave enough yarn to sew the tail to the body.

Large horns (x2)

Use red yarn.

Round 1: 6 sc (*UK dc*) in magic ring (6 sts).

Round 2: 1 sc (*UK dc*) in each st to end.

Round 3: *1 sc (*UK dc*) in next st, 2 sc (*UK dc*) in next st; rep from * to end (9 sts).

Rounds 4 and 5: As Round 2.

Round 6: *1 sc (*UK dc*) in next 2 sts, 2 sc (*UK dc*) in next st; rep from * to end (12 sts).

Rounds 7 and 8: As Round 2.

Round 9: *1 sc (*UK dc*) in next 3 sts, 2 sc (*UK dc*) in next st; rep from * to end (15 sts).

Round 10: As Round 2.

Fill the horns. Tie off with a sl st, and leave enough yarn to sew the horns to the head.

Small horns (x2)

Use red yarn.

Work Rounds 1–7 as for large horns.

Fill the horns. Tie off with a sl st, and leave enough yarn to sew the horns to the head.

Wings (x4)

Use yellow yarn. At the end of each row turn work.

Row 1: 1 ch + 1 tch.

Row 2: Skip tch, 2 sc (*UK dc*) in next ch (2 sts).

Row 3: 1 tch, 1 sc (*UK dc*) in each st to last st, 2 sc (*UK dc*) in last st (3 sts).

Row 4: 1 tch, 2 sc (*UK dc*) in next st, 1 sc (*UK dc*) in each st to end (4 sts).

Rows 5 and 6: As Rows 3 and 4 (6 sts).

Row 7: 1 tch, 1 sc (*UK dc*) in each st to last 2 sts, dec over last 2 sts (5 sts).

Row 8: 1 tch, dec over next 2 sts, 1 sc (*UK dc*) in each st to end (4 sts).

Row 9: As Row 3 (5 sts).

Row 10: As Row 8 (4 sts).

Row 11: 1 tch, [dec over next 2 sts] twice (2 sts).

Row 12: 1 tch, 1 sc (*UK dc*) in each st to end.

Tie off. Hold 2 wing pieces together and work a row of sc (*UK dc*) around entire edge to join. Repeat for other wing. Leave enough yarn to sew the wings to the body.

Work one row of sc (*UK dc*) with red yarn along the top edge of each wing. Leave enough yarn to sew the wings to the body.

Putting all the parts together

Sew the body to the head, at approximately Round 9.

Sew the large horns to the head, at approximately Round 15. Sew the small horns next to them at approximately Round 16.

Sew the belly to the body, approximately 2 rounds below neck.

Sew the arms to the body, approximately 3 rounds below neck.

Sew the feet to the legs and then sew the legs to the body, approximately 7 rounds below neck.

Sew the tail to the body, approximately 8 rounds below neck.

For the flames, attach 4 orange and 4 yellow acrylic strands of yarn to the end of the tail. To do this, double each strand of yarn, push hook through a single stitch, yarn over, then pull the tail end through the stitch to form a knot. Cut the yarn, leaving the attached strands at a length approximately 4cm (1^1/$_2$in) long. Brush them to make them fluffy.

Sew the wings to the body, at approximately Round 3, with 1 stitch between the wings.

Face

Cut 2 eyes out of white and black felt and paste these onto the head, at approximately Round 8.

For a complete list of all our books see

www.searchpress.com